"For educators, parents and community activists who recognize that schools can't address the needs of students without support, this book will be a tremendous asset and an invaluable resource. Throughout the book, Emily Woods provides us with insights into how to devise a strategy to create and sustain community schools. Filled with quotes and stories from people who have led this work, the book is practical, insightful, and most of all, inspirational."

Pedro A. Noguera, *Distinguished Professor of Education, USC Rossier School of Education, USA.*

"Community schools are a strategy for all schools. *Making Community Schools a Reality* will serve an anchor for principals ready to expand their leadership and make their schools a holistic center for students, families and communities. While the pages of this book speak directly to principals, teachers and community school practitioners, anyone in education would benefit from the best-practices and wisdom presented."

Amy Ellis, *Director of the Center for Community Schools, University of Central Florida, USA.*

"*Making Community Schools a Reality* serves as both a practical guide and a call to action for educators, policymakers, and community leaders, offering a blueprint for creating schools that address the non-traditional needs of students and families. Woods reinforces the idea that education is not only about what happens in the classroom, but how schools can drive long-term, transformative change through collaboration, fostering stronger, healthier communities."

Richard M. Gordon IV, *Assistant Superintendent, School District of Philadelphia, USA.*

"Finally, a resource that combines principals' wisdom with evidence-based strategies to successfully implement and lead community schools. In this book, Woods takes the reader through a series of steps needed to create conditions that address school/community readiness, foster collaboration, and develop an infrastructure to support the community school strategy. Unlike other books in the field, *Making Community Schools a Reality: Harnessing the Power of School Leaders* anticipates the challenges faced by principals and delivers concrete solutions to navigate their community school journey."

JoAnne Ferrara, *Professor Emerita, Manhattanville University, USA.*

"Emily Woods has written a useful and valuable book that will help the range of community schools advocates and practitioners to better comprehend the significance of the work for children, families, communities, and society."

Ira Harkavy, *Founding Director of the Netter Center for Community Partnerships, University of Pennsylvania, USA.*

Making Community Schools a Reality

With public demand for community schools on the rise, this timely book provides an empowering, step-by-step approach for school leaders to cultivate community school practices within their schools while simultaneously engaging in the policy advocacy process. This is an actionable toolkit with practical advice, helpful checklists and inventories, as well as real examples from rural and urban schools. Drawing from the experiences of real school leaders involved in community school initiatives, this book illuminates the promise of community schools as centers of the community and sites accessible beyond regular school hours. Community schools bring together educators, local community members, families, and students to provide partnerships that strengthen conditions for student learning and healthy development. *Making Community Schools a Reality* is a timely and comprehensive resource that helps educational leaders improve learning outcomes and promote equity in their schools.

Emily L. Woods is a former K-12 teacher and teacher trainer. She is currently Director of Education for the Richard K. Lubin Family Foundation, where she advances the benefits of community schools in urban public education. She has also served as Adjunct Lecturer in UMass Boston's Education Leadership doctoral program.

Also Available from Routledge Eye on Education
(www.routledge.com/eyeoneducation)

Culturally Conscious Decision-Making for School Leaders: A Toolkit for Creating a More Equitable School Culture
Shauna McGee

Coaching Education Leaders: A Culturally Responsive Approach to Transforming Schools and Systems
Nancy B. Gutiérrez, Michelle Jarney, and Michael Kim

Fostering Parent Engagement for Equitable and Successful SchoolsA Leader's Guide to Supporting Families and Students
Patrick Darfler-Sweeney

Finding Your Path as a Woman in School Leadership: A Guide for Educators, Allies, and Advocates
Kim Cofino and Christina Botbyl

A Leadership Playbook for Addressing Rapid Change in Education: Empowered for Success
Teresa L. San Martín

Improving Teacher Morale and Motivation: Leadership Strategies that Build Student Success
Ronald Williamson and Barbara R. Blackburn

Lead with Truth: How to Make a Difference in Your School, Your Life, and the Lives of Your Students
Qiana O'Leary

When Black Students Excel: How Schools Can Engage and Empower Black Students
Joseph F. Johnson, Jr., Cynthia L. Uline, and Stanley J. Munro, Jr.

Making Community Schools a Reality

Harnessing Your Power as a School Leader through Collaboration

Emily L. Woods

NEW YORK AND LONDON

Cover image: © Getty Images

First published 2025
by Routledge
605 Third Avenue, New York, NY 10158

and by Routledge
4 Park Square, Milton Park, Abingdon, Oxon, OX14 4RN

Routledge is an imprint of the Taylor & Francis Group, an informa business

© 2025 Emily L. Woods

The right of Emily L. Woods to be identified as author of this work has been asserted in accordance with sections 77 and 78 of the Copyright, Designs and Patents Act 1988.

All rights reserved. No part of this book may be reprinted or reproduced or utilised in any form or by any electronic, mechanical, or other means, now known or hereafter invented, including photocopying and recording, or in any information storage or retrieval system, without permission in writing from the publishers.

Trademark notice: Product or corporate names may be trademarks or registered trademarks, and are used only for identification and explanation without intent to infringe.

Library of Congress Cataloging-in-Publication Data
Names: Woods, Emily (Emily Lubin), author.
Title: Making community schools a reality : harnessing your power as a school leader through collaboration / Emily L. Woods.
Description: New York, NY : Routledge, 2025. | Includes bibliographical references and index.
Identifiers: LCCN 2025000846 (print) | LCCN 2025000847 (ebook) | ISBN 9781032717685 (hardback) | ISBN 9781032717692 (paperback) | ISBN 9781032693101 (ebook)
Subjects: LCSH: Community schools.
Classification: LCC LB2820 .W65 2025 (print) | LCC LB2820 (ebook) | DDC 371.03--dc23/eng/20250225
LC record available at https://lccn.loc.gov/2025000846
LC ebook record available at https://lccn.loc.gov/2025000847

ISBN: 9781032717685 (hbk)
ISBN: 9781032693101 (pbk)
ISBN: 9781032717692 (ebk)

DOI: 10.4324/9781032717692

Typeset in Palatino
by KnowledgeWorks Global Ltd.

Contents

Foreword by Jane Quinn viii
Preface by Emily L. Woods. xi
Acknowledgments by Emily L. Woods. xiv

1 Introduction. 1

2 Understanding the "What" and "Why" of Community Schools 21

3 Creating a State of Readiness 40

4 Realizing the Vision by Developing and Enhancing Systems and Structures. 62

5 Building a Sound Foundation: Data, Evaluation, and Funding 95

6 The Principal's Role in Advocating for Change. 122

7 Making It Work: A Question of Equity 143

Appendix A. Stages of Development. 156
Appendix B. Path to a Vision: Oyler School,
    Cincinnati Ohio (Pre K-12) 157
Appendix C. Assets and Needs Assessment Toolkit 159
Appendix D. Community Schools Communications Toolkit . . . 164
Index 170

Foreword

Jane Quinn[1]

This is a book that was itching to be written.

The growing literature on community schools as a preferred education reform strategy offers many strengths but also suffers from at least one major gap: the all-important role of the principal in community school implementation. Emily Woods has courageously and respectfully stepped into this breach, bringing her incisive analytical skills and strong policy orientation—both of which are represented in her earlier book as well, *The Path to Successful Community School Policy Adoption: A Comparative Analysis of District-Level Policy Reform Processes* (Routledge, 2023).

The critical role of the principal in K-12 school improvement has long been recognized, thanks in no small measure to the work of Anthony Bryk and his colleagues at the Consortium for Chicago School Research. The 2010 publication of their landmark study, *Organizing Schools for Improvement: Lessons from Chicago*,[2,3] garnered a front-page story in *Education Week* as well as wide interest in the world of K-12 education. The Bryk team spent nearly two decades studying 200 elementary schools in Chicago, 100 of which had improved steadily, and an equal number whose achievement results had plateaued or declined. The research team sought to understand what factors mattered most for improving student achievement in these low-income urban schools.

Their conclusion was startling in its clarity: improving schools requires coherent, orchestrated action across five essential supports. The first of these five key ingredients is a form of principal leadership that drives change and employs an inclusive approach. The four other supports include student-centered school climate, attention to building faculty and staff capacity, coherent and consistent instructional guidance, and authentic family and community engagement. The Bryk team compares these five essential ingredients of school improvement to the butter, sugar, eggs, flour, and baking powder that are the core of any cake recipe. No ingredient can be left out, and the interaction among them accounts for the success (or failure) of the enterprise.

Organizing Schools for Improvement emphasizes the centrality of inclusive principal leadership as the driver of school-based change. In a journal article outlining the book's key ideas, Bryk wrote:

> Principals in improving schools engage in a dynamic interplay of instructional and inclusive-facilitative leadership. On the instructional side, school leaders influence local activity around core instructional programs, supplemental academic and social supports, and the hiring and development of staff. They establish strategic priorities for using resources and buffer externalities that might distract from coherent reform. Working in tandem with this, principals build relationships across the school community. Improving teaching and learning places demands on these relationships. In carrying out their daily activities, school leaders advance instrumental objectives while also trying to enlist teachers in the change effort. In the process, principals cultivate a growing cadre of leaders (teachers, parents, and community members) who can help expand the reach of this work and share overall responsibility for improvement.[4]

The Bryk team's analysis centered on, and took advantage of, district-wide changes resulting from the passage of the Chicago School Reform Act of 1988, which supported site-based decision-making through Local School Councils and principal autonomy. Although the Chicago Public Schools later adopted the community school strategy as a major reform effort, the Bryk study was launched well before the community school initiative, and it did not focus on the community school strategy per se, although it is likely that some of the schools included in the study participated in both initiatives.

That said, the relevance of the Bryk analysis to the work of community schools is clear: improving schools requires the very elements that are central to the community school strategy, such as strong parent-community-school ties and student-centered learning environments.

The rigor and scope of the Bryk team's analysis generated interest across the K-12 education field and created demand for additional resources on how to translate this solid empirical evidence into daily practice. The continued growth of the community school field over the past decade has led to the development of new frameworks, tools, implementation guides, playbooks, sustainability manuals, and research syntheses. Missing from this catalog, until now, has been a resource focused specifically on principal leadership in community schools.

With this volume, Emily Woods ventured into this fertile ground by interviewing over 40 community school leaders in locations across the country and combining those results with an astute analysis of relevant literature on topics as diverse as vision-setting, equity, sustainability, systems, structures, and evaluation. The author and her interviewees rightly call attention to the non-negotiable elements of the community school strategy, such as conducting systematic needs and assets assessments at the building level and nurturing strong partnerships between principals and community school coordinators/directors. Another salient aspect of the book is the decided emphasis on the role of the principal as an advocate for policy change at multiple levels, including district, city, state, and federal.

Woods writes with energy and compassion as her informants discuss the complexity of their responsibilities, the strength of their convictions, and the depth of their expertise. This book serves as a useful reminder that the work of improving practice should rely heavily on the wisdom of practitioners—the unsung heroes (and heroines) who staff and lead our nation's public schools.

Preface

Emily L. Woods

Since the publication of my book, *The Path to Successful Community School Adoption* (Routledge, 2022), the call for community schools has grown louder and more urgent. City and school district leaders increasingly recognize the transformative potential of community schools as a strategy to improve learning outcomes in historically underserved schools. Designed to function as vibrant hubs for their neighborhoods, community schools engage students, families, teachers, and local organizations in a collaborative effort to provide coordinated educational, health, and social support services. Open on evenings, weekends, and summers, these schools become anchors in their communities. In the wake of the pandemic, this initiative has gained unprecedented momentum, with districts across the country—from New York City to Cincinnati and Oakland—adopting community schools as a key pathway to academic success. States including Kentucky, California, and West Virginia are embracing community schools as part of their long-term education reform strategies, and federal funding has quadrupled since 2018.

While my earlier research focused on policy, I came to see the critical role that school leaders play in bringing community schools to life. My findings underscored that the success of community schools was enhanced by the ability of school leaders to advocate for their schools and mobilize their communities, even amid setbacks and leadership transitions. Yet, resources for principals and other school leaders on the front lines of educational change remained scarce.

When my publisher suggested writing a book specifically for school leaders, I was initially hesitant to shift my focus from policy. However, as I reflected on the impact of effective community school leaders across the country, I realized the transformative potential of such a resource. This book is the result.

Making Community Schools a Reality: Harnessing the Power of School Leaders addresses the vital role of principals, assistant principals, and other leaders within community schools. It provides an actionable toolkit to help develop community school practices, advocate for supportive policies, and prepare schools and districts to embrace this powerful initiative. Drawing from the experiences of over 40 school leaders involved in community school initiatives, the book combines their successes, challenges, and lessons learned with my own research and professional background. Together, these perspectives offer a comprehensive guide for school leaders ready to transform their schools into thriving community schools.

The book's opening chapter presents the rationale for why community schools are an essential reform strategy to meet the needs of today's educational challenges and outlines some of the skills and characteristics of successful community school leaders. Chapter 2 continues to lay the foundation, defining key terms, outlining essential components, and tracing the evolution of community schools. This chapter also discusses common fears associated with implementing and growing this transformative approach. Chapter 3 then turns to the important work of creating a shared vision, highlighting the importance of collaborative leadership in bringing the shared vision to life. Chapter 4 provides a practical roadmap for establishing several key systems and structures to realize the school's vision, including designating a high-level community school coordinator, conducting a needs and assets assessment, forming intentional and integrated partnerships, and enhancing authentic parent engagement. Chapter 5 focuses on data, evaluation, and funding strategies for community schools and explains how to use a logic model to track key data, align stakeholders, and create an action plan. Chapter 5 also underscores the importance of a strong financial foundation using Deich and Neary's funding framework and stresses the value of diverse data, including qualitative measures, to evaluate success beyond traditional academic metrics. Chapter 6 elevates the school leader's role in the community school advocacy process, mobilizing a diverse range of stakeholders to deliver compelling messages about the value of community schools. The book concludes with an exploration of community schools as a vehicle for achieving a more just educational system. This chapter also presents a series of questions for school leaders to self-assess their ability to maintain an asset-based approach.

While each chapter is filled with the voices of principals, they all conclude with a targeted question posed to principals in the field. These responses provide readers with practical insights and diverse perspectives of experienced community school leaders, enabling readers to reflect on real-world applications and challenges within the context of the chapter's themes.

I wrote this book as a call to action for school leaders to broaden their community school strategies, harness their influence, and become champions of community schools. While the primary audience is intended to be school leaders, any community school practitioner or stakeholder will find the book useful for improving their own practices in and support of their community school. By equipping leaders with the tools and knowledge they need, I aim to contribute to a growing movement with the potential to reshape education across the United States.

Notes

1. Jane Quinn, Ph.D., directed the Children's Aid National Center for Community Schools from 2000 to 2018. She is the co-author of three books on community schools, including the 2023 volume entitled *The Community Schools Revolution: Building Partnerships, Transforming Lives, Advancing Democracy.*
2. Bryk, A. S. (2010). Organizing schools for improvement. *Phi delta kappan, 91*(7), 23-30.
3. Bryk, J. S., Sebring, P. B., Allensworth, E., Luppescu, S., and Easton, J. Q. (2010).
4. Bryk, J. S., "Organizing Schools for Improvement," *Kappan,* 91(7), p. 25.

Acknowledgments

Emily L. Woods

My most heartfelt thanks goes to all of the principals, former principals, and district superintendents who participated in my research and taught me far more about their work and craft than I could ever have imagined. What an honor it has been to learn from you.

A huge thank you to the coordinators and coordinator supervisors who lost hours of their lives explaining the landscape from their perspective: Migdalia Cortes, Dante DeTablan. and Jo Gomes.

I am grateful to the community school experts who were willing to explore every nuance of community schools with me and indulge my endless questions: Jay Roscup, Stacey Campo, Luan Kida, and JoAnne Ferrara (who, beyond a shadow of a doubt, definitely DNS!).

I'm so fortunate to have had some really wise academics to guide my path, including Kathleen Provinzano, Jerry Johnson, Amy Ellis, and James Coviello, whose imprints are all over this book.

To my army of unpaid and overworked readers and editors, including the tireless Janice Woods, who may have read the whole book six times, Nancy Lubin, Amy Barkan, Rebecca Nordhaus, Margaret Lawrence, Jenn Krebs, and Joelle Boucai (via Kate the incomparable): I am profoundly thankful.

While some might say she's the godmother of community schools, Jane Quinn is really and truly my own fairy godmother. This book would not have been possible without her.

To Greg and my girls, thank you for your support, patience, and your heroic efforts to keep the guilt trips to a minimum.

And finally, to my wolf pack and sister wives who got me across the finish line.

1
Introduction

Why This? Why Now?

> During my time as assistant principal and then principal, I've been a part of so many great initiatives. I've been part of expeditionary learning, I've been part of International Baccalaureate, and I've worked through many different literacy models that have come and gone. With all of these models, there's a lot of hope. And change did happen to some degree, but it wasn't until I went through this experience of transforming into a community school that I saw change that's going to last, that's really going to make a difference. The instructional pieces that I learned through some of those more academic models were great and important. But community schools represent the kind of transformation and progress that is going to have a lasting impact—especially for the students who need it the most.
> Ann Hanna, *Community School Consultant in the Maine Department of Education and Former Principal at Gerald E. Talbot Community School, Portland, ME*

> Community schools are about the basics. At the core, the number one goal is removing barriers to learning. And that doesn't look the same for every child. The first misconception is that community schools isn't about getting back to the basics. It is. The 'basics' is learning. Community schools help everybody do just that.
> Sandi Calvin, *Associate Superintendent of Union Public Schools (Tulsa and Broken Arrow, Oklahoma)*

I'm going to go out on a limb here. My best guess is that it would be hard to find a principal who, at one point or the other, has not fallen victim to the initiative-itis that Principal Hanna described. It feels like a given that every so often, a new shiny (often wonderful, but sometimes not) initiative comes along, whether a new math program, a partnership with a university for mental health services, or a novel way of structuring instructional time. Many long-standing principals have also lived through more sweeping reforms and programs such as *No Child Left Behind* and *Race to the Top*. Yet, the achievement gap is still widening. Systemic socioeconomic and racial disparities still remain, and they wreak havoc on students' educational experiences. There is, however, a solution that has proven to create better student outcomes: community schools.

Community schools are not a shiny new object, nor are they a piecemeal program. They are an evidenced-based, comprehensive set of strategies that have thrived across the United States for decades. Community schools recognize that schools can no longer work in isolation, solely focused on teaching and learning, without acknowledging the powerful factors that exist outside the classroom.

Those coming into this work with little background knowledge about community schools might be wondering what exactly they are. In a nutshell, community schools are public schools that become hubs for students and communities. Often open evenings and over weekends and summers, they build partnerships with families, students, teachers, and local organizations—ideally the whole community—to identify and provide health, social, instructional, and out of school time support. The entire school community shares their priorities and then determines an action plan in which resources and relationships align toward achieving this shared vision.

The late Patricia Harvey, former superintendent of St. Paul Public Schools, described community schools in one pithy sentence:

> Community schools are a strategy for organizing the resources of the school and community around student success.

While it is short and to the point, there are several notable elements here. The first is that Superintendent Harvey was careful to describe community schools as a strategy—not a program. This is an important distinction, especially because we have all been conditioned to think in terms of programs, services, and interventions. Unlike a program, community schools are a strategy that is flexible and evolving. They change over time, often integrating existing and new partners, and use funding from a variety of sources.[1] Community schools are multi-faceted and adaptive, and they require lots of different people to inform and drive the solutions they generate.

Many people think of schools as something analogous to a traditional land-line phone—a simple, two-way system of delivery where teachers teach and students learn. Community schools are more like smartphones. They use high-level systems and structures that help educators and community members work together to pool resources, think more expansively, and ultimately be able to "open the right app at the right time."

But let's go back to the idea of community schools being a strategy, not a program. It is important to stress that programs, services, and interventions are necessary components of community schools. We *need* high-quality programs and services. Community schools create the connective tissue among those programs, if you will, as well as the decision-making processes that make them most relevant and best-utilized. Therefore, perhaps an even truer version of the definition above is as follows:

> Community schools are a strategy that organizes the resources *and the voices* of the school and community around student success.

The end goal? Well, as Superintendent Calvin explained, it is to remove barriers to learning—to ensure open pathways to academic success. And as we will see, doing this work systemically is nothing less than a whole new way of doing school.

The Rationale for Community Schools: The Pandemic and Before

By way of a brief history lesson, the Coleman Report, published in the 1960s, made it clear that a child's socioeconomic background and status were more important contributors to academic outcomes than any amount of school-based funding.[2] More recent research has confirmed that conclusion. Six out-of-school factors, including subpar medical care and food insecurity, are clearly shown to limit children's potential for academic growth and speak to the fact that schools alone cannot compensate for what happens outside of the school walls.[3] Researchers argue that such external factors account for as much as two-thirds of the difference in academic outcomes.[4]

Schools have almost no choice but to provide social supports,[5] despite the fact that school reforms typically fail to address challenges such as poverty and lack of equitable access to resources. The late Jeannie Oakes, a prominent scholar in the field of educational equity, offers that,

> The school and its community [must create a] coherent ecology in which schools have a crucial, but not sole responsibility for teaching and social betterment.[6]

Another way of understanding Oakes's argument is by contrasting the idea of a "coherent ecology" with what some refer to as a "technical" reform approach. A technical approach ignores all out-of-school factors. Instead, it views poor educational outcomes as a sole function of failures within school systems, including (but not limited to) subpar teaching, weak curriculum, low standards, and too much bureaucracy, among others.[7] While these technical areas may be in need of serious attention, the solely technical approach to tackling the challenges facing school districts stands in sharp contrast to the more complex, often bolder, and more comprehensive reform approaches that community schools represent.[8]

While the need to ensure open pathways to academic success by moving beyond a technical approach to school reform existed long before the COVID-19 pandemic, that crisis certainly didn't help. As we all well know, it exacerbated health and wellness disparities, food insecurity, housing challenges, and a digital divide. The pandemic demanded that we think about education reform differently. Instead of reform being something administrators and school boards insist must be done to kids, we now see reform as something that entire communities, especially those that are the most disenfranchised, can make decisions about together.

During the pandemic, because many community schools had local partnerships in place, they were better able to serve the needs of their families than non-community schools. They were able to help with childcare, with providing food and clothing, and by ensuring access to the technology required for students to participate in virtual school.

Post-pandemic, all schools must continue to address those same basic needs while contending with waning federal funds and the ongoing heightened challenges of dropout rates, low levels of student engagement, and homelessness. Chronic absenteeism, defined as when students miss more than 10% of school per year, is another major issue. Simply put, if students are not in school, they cannot learn. Chronic absenteeism is becoming an issue that if not addressed, and not met with a comprehensive approach, will become a true crisis for our youth and our entire society as a whole.

Community schools are a strategy that strikes directly at the heart of chronic absenteeism, as well as so many other issues (e.g. drop-out rates, student engagement, and homelessness). The partnerships central to community schools and the relationship building inherent in such an approach is exactly what is required to get kids to school and enable them to thrive once back in the classroom.

The Growing Call for Community Schools

It is not surprising that calls for community schools are growing louder and more frequent. Federal data has shown a huge spike in community schools. In fact, as of 2023, more than half of public schools in the United States are using many, if not all, aspects of a community schools approach.[9] Communities, both rural and urban e.g. (NYC, Cincinnati, Deer River, MN, and Kern County, CA), are adopting this initiative at the local level. States, both red and blue, are making significant investments in community schools. Notably, California has invested $4.1 billion over seven years to establish the California Community Schools Partnership Grant Program, with the intention of making every high-poverty school in California a community school.[10] Maryland has invested $116.9 million in their community schools, more than double that of FY 2021.[11] Florida has increased its investment each year since 2014, including an allocation of $20.1 million in 2024 for community school planning, implementation, technical assistance, and certification of staff.[12] Other states such as Georgia, Illinois, Kentucky, New Mexico, Florida, and New York also made significant investments in state-level funding or invested in capacity building for community school initiatives.[13]

Some states have even established comprehensive community school legislation. For example, in Maryland, MD S 661 codifies and defines community schools in the state and explicitly states their nonnegotiable elements (e.g. community schools must have a community school coordinator and leadership team, and they must establish a community school leadership team to conduct a needs and assets assessment that will inform the implementation plan).[14]

At the federal level, in 2023, President Biden dedicated $150 million for the Full-Service Community Schools program–double its size from 2022 and quadruple its size from 2018.

The increase in the sheer number of community schools and local, state, and national investment is, of course, driven by need. But community schools are backed by data, meaning they've got a proven track record. A number of studies have pointed to improved outcomes in areas such as attendance; chronic absenteeism; high school graduation rates; perceptions of school climate by teachers, parents, and students; and reductions in disciplinary incidents. Such outcomes often translate into direct academic outcomes. In fact, a 2017 study (Learning Policy Institute and National Education Policy Center) synthesized findings from 143 rigorous evaluations of the component parts of community schools. It concluded that well-implemented community schools reduce barriers to learning and help at-risk students succeed academically—especially low-income students that attend high-poverty schools.[15]

Other studies have found economic benefits to community school strategies, in the form of Return on Investment (ROI) data. These studies, including a 2013 study conducted by the Finance Project, a 2012 study performed by Economic Modeling Specialists Inc., and a 2019 study commissioned by the ABC Community School partnership in Albuquerque, found that for every $1 invested in student supports at community schools, the community school coordinator position itself, and other types of community school programming yielded between a $7–$14 return on investment.[16]

And finally, an important study from 2020, led by the RAND corporation, examined community schools in New York City. This study found academic, attendance, graduation, and climate and culture gains (see Chapter 6 for more details). Clearly, the benefits of transforming schools into community schools make it easy to decide to take the leap. So, the question isn't "Should I encourage my school to become a community school?" but "How do I get my school to transition to a community school?"

What's Your Starting Point?

While I hope this book is of service to a diverse range of people interested in community schools, principals are the primary audience.

Before starting this book, it's important to pause, just for a moment, and acknowledge two things: first where you are in the lifespan of a principal, and second, the space you inhabit along the community school journey.

You may be a new, or fairly new principal, or you may be a seasoned veteran. You may have no experience with a community school, your school may possess several of the qualities of a community school, or you may have lived the community school experience for some time now.

Your school may also have become a community school in different ways. It may be a top-down approach (district- or state-mandated) or bottom-up approach (school- and educator-driven).

Your school might have been recently designated a community school by the district or state (top-down); your district may have recently received a federal community school grant (typically top-down); you may have sought out this approach yourself (bottom-up); or you are an existing community school that knows that it can do even more to support its students and families (either top-down or bottom-up). Or it may even be a "joint initiative," where the school in conjunction with the school district works together to launch a true community school.[17]

Wherever you are in this principal and community school journey, my best advice is to learn as much as you can—whether from this book, from exemplary principals and coordinators in your district and beyond, from national and regional technical assistance centers, or from the growing number of case studies of best practices that are emerging in real time. I cannot stress enough that the path to community school excellence is ongoing. There is always room to strengthen practice.

Additionally, in the mid-1990s, a "Stages of Development Tool"[18] was created by the National Center for Community Schools, which was more recently updated by a national community school coalition called Community Schools Forward.[19] This tool maps different areas of community school development: the emerging stage, the maturing stage, and the transforming stage (see Appendix A). As the coalition suggests, community schools are a long-term strategy, and the path is not linear. Different areas may be further developed than others, and challenges and setbacks can derail even the best of plans. So, wherever you are in your principal journey, and wherever you are in your community school development (even if at the VERY beginning), be patient. Be curious. As I have learned in researching this book, it's about the long game.

I Don't Have Time for One More Thing!

Being a principal is one of the most rewarding jobs in the world. It can also be one of the most demanding. According to a survey by the RAND Corporation, principals are twice as likely to describe their job as inducing high levels of stress, compared to adults in different professions. In fact, this survey found that principals reported experiencing frequent job stress even more than teachers did.[20]

The challenges that principals face are vast. The day doesn't end at 3:00. Or 5:00. Or ever, really. The hours are long. The principal's role is often reactive, where it sometimes feels as though they spend the majority of their time responding to each urgent crisis as it arises, whether it's handling student discipline incidents, meeting students' mental health needs, managing security and safely protocols, or calming upset parents. This can mean that principals have less time than they'd like to collaborate with school staff, gather with parents and community members, and spend on long-term strategic planning.

There is also a great deal of pressure and accountability—from the district, state, and parents. There is often a tremendous feeling of powerlessness in the face of all needs to be done with limited time and resources to make things happen. And there is often burnout.

The community school strategies outlined in this book are designed to help principals catch their breath and break free from the spiral of reactive leadership. It won't happen right away, and it won't be a straight line. But ultimately, the investment will be worth it—both for you as principal, and for the entire community that you serve.

Am I the Right Person for This Job?

In the process of researching the book, I talked with many individuals steeped in the community school experience, interviewing over 40 school leaders (urban and rural), as well as professors, think-tank leaders, and technical assistance providers. This research was essential in giving me real-world understanding of issues around community schools, which I also researched for my dissertation and first book. One urban principal provided this important context:

The principal wears many hats regardless of what school he or she is in, most importantly that of instructional leader. But being the principal of a community school involves broadening your lens, thinking about the whole child, and building systems and structures. Leading a community school is an exercise in shared leadership and decision-making. It isn't a natural approach for many, but it is a core component of a community school. And if you're ready to embrace the strategy, because you know it's a strategy that can transform your school, not because you're told to do so or because there is a pot of money available, I urge you to be willing to adapt as a leader and go all in.

What does it mean to be a principal who is ready to "go all in" on community schools? What types of qualities must a principal believe in ... and embody? These qualities might include that of an entrepreneur, risk taker, expert listener, problem solver, community organizer, relationship-builder, cross boundary leader, and systems thinker. But it needs to be said that many (if not all) great principals personify a good number of these characteristics without even knowing it, whether their school is a community school or not. Yet, for some, many of the terms listed above are outside their comfort zone, particularly the last two: cross-boundary leadership and being a systems thinker. Let's dig into them now, as they are perhaps the most complicated.

Cross-Boundary Leader

This sounds like a very fancy term. But what it's really saying is that community school principals must work around and across traditional boundaries. The Coalition for Community Schools developed this term and highlighted that cross-boundary leadership, empowering and mobilizing leaders at all sorts of different levels (both inside and outside of school walls), "lies at the heart of community schools."[21]

There are two main elements of being a cross-boundary principal.[22] The first is that of being the conductor, orchestrator, magician (pick your metaphor) in charge of the vision for the work. But, this broad vision is not just the vision for the school itself. It's a vision for the school *and* the community together. It is orchestrated by the principal but owned by both.

The second element is the role the principal plays in bringing together different groups of leaders. Marty Blank,[23] one of top community school gurus, described three different levels of leaders that cross boundary leadership must encompass: community leadership, leadership on the ground, and leadership in the middle.

- Community leaders: These are the leaders within the school district and the city offices, and the broader business and nonprofit community.
- Leaders on the ground: These are school leaders and staff—principals, teachers, community members, and the community school coordinator (we will get to that in the next chapter for those who are unfamiliar with the term).
- Leaders in the middle: These are the nonprofit directors or coordinators of local community groups.

While perhaps the role of the principal traditionally has been to focus on their school staff (i.e. leaders on the ground), the cross-boundary leader is able to work across—to develop relationships across, build trust across—these three different levels of leadership. The cross-boundary leader can navigate all three and bring leaders from all three groups together in pursuit of a shared vision.

Systems Thinker

Systems thinking is a way of seeing and creating a complex web of interconnected parts. The most important part of the system is not the individual components—but rather the relationship among them. The parts need to work together in order for the entire system to thrive,[24] and parts need to be seen in relationship to the whole. Systems thinking pervades the world of any principal, but it is especially heightened in the community school context.

The Oxfam organization emphasizes systems thinking in relationship to the onboarding of staff and development practitioners.

These three essential elements are closely aligned with the tenets of community schools[25]:

- Collaboration across organizational boundaries, incorporating diverse ideas and perspectives.
- The prioritization of context-specific solutions over generic approaches drawn from best practices in other settings.
- A focus on the development and deployment of complex resources.

With systems thinking, educators and school leaders must be able to collaborate across organizational boundaries; they must be a cross-boundary leader. They must also consider the broader systemic factors impacting students' lives and use a variety of resources in response.

As explained by Chris Coan, principal at Parker Elementary, Panama City, Florida,

> I am constantly thinking about what my final product is—which is always about what is best for the families and what is best for the community. With the final product in mind, I'm then asking myself if I am doing it strategically. Because yes, maybe you address one community thing, but then there's seven more coming down the pike. I am always questioning, "Are the decisions that we're making impacting one? Or are the decisions impacting many?" If the decisions are truly impacting many, then you're not just filling a hole—you're getting at the systemic principles. But I can't stress enough—that not one person can be the change agent. It must be a whole ecosystem working together.

In a community school, systems and structures are designed to disrupt the fragmentation and "one-offs" so often exhibited when schools provide services and learning supports. Instead, the goal is to get at the root causes of problems, not just the "quick fix" solutions.

In addition, systems thinking in a community school pushes on traditional boundaries. In many schools, an individual teacher's responsibility is solely the students in their classroom. The classroom itself is a system—a fairly complicated one at that. But in a community school, the system becomes exponentially bigger. Teachers are part of a system where they work collaboratively with all staff members, including leadership, support personnel, and external partners to work toward a shared vision. The entire school community has "skin in the game" and a vested interest in the performance of the school as a whole. By adopting systems thinking, community schools transform into interconnected, adaptive ecosystems. They embrace the complexity of the challenges they face, leveraging collaboration and data to create meaningful, sustainable change. In a community school, the system includes the school and the community that surrounds it. In fact, members from the whole community come together to establish common priorities, goals, and outcomes and then work collaboratively to get there.

Now that we have covered these two topics, we will discuss the wide range of leadership skills needed to implement systems thinking effectively.

Leadership—A Three-Skill Approach

Many really smart people have tried to explain or conceptualize great leadership. One of them is Robert Katz, who wrote about a three-skill approach to leadership in a 2009 Harvard Business Review article. What he meant is that being a great leader was dependent on three different types of skills: conceptual skills, technical skills, and human skills.

Conceptual skills have to do with setting a vision and providing strategic direction. Technical skills refer to specific knowledge that you have in a given area. Human skills are about relating to and communicating with other people.

Let's think about these three skills for a school leader through a negative lens. Even if a leader has an unbelievable vision for the work ahead, if they cannot communicate it to others and no one wants to be on board, this leader cannot be effective. Even if the leader is the most charismatic, the most motivating human ever, if they don't have a strong understanding of teaching and learning, or curriculum, or the evaluation process, or they have trouble utilizing data for school improvement, this engaging human will not be effective in their leadership role. Let's say the leader really gets teaching and learning and is *so* well versed in the curriculum, but when a major problem arises, they cannot analyze the situation and provide high-level strategic direction to move the school through and forward—they also cannot be truly effective.

In short, community school leaders must have all three skills. They must be able to see the path forward for the school. They must create a vision for the work and a strategic action plan that involves not just the school community—but the entire community that surrounds the school—that "systems thinking" we heard about earlier. This is an example of the highest level of conceptual thinking.

What You Will Find in This Book

The first two chapters provide a foundational understanding of the community schools strategy by defining key terms, outlining essential components, and discussing the evolution of community schools. School leaders will gain insights into the leadership skills necessary for success, including systems thinking and cross-boundary leadership, along with practical guidance on navigating the challenges and fears associated with implementing this transformative approach. These chapters are important, even for veteran leaders, as they may help principals stay informed about the evolving community school landscape and ensure common language throughout the remainder of the book.

Chapters 3 and 4 are about creating a shared vision and establishing several key systems and structures that underpin a thriving community school. Chapter 3 explores the collaboratively developed vision, one that involves stakeholders such as parents, students, and community members, and fosters ownership and buy-in, ensuring the vision's sustainability. This chapter also explores the importance of transitioning to a collaborative leadership model, where all members of the community contribute to realizing the vision, leading to more effective and enduring results.

Chapter 4 provides a practical roadmap for establishing several key systems and structures. Such elements include understanding the crucial role of the community school coordinator, mastering the needs and assets assessment process, building a strong network of integrated partners, and moving from a more transactional model of parent involvement to one that supports more authentic parent engagement.

For seasoned leaders, these chapters can validate existing practices and highlight areas for strengthening community school initiatives.

Chapter 5 shifts the focus to data, evaluation and funding. It emphasizes that a strong financial foundation is essential for community schools, urging school leaders to implement strategies such as integrating and aligning funds to secure diverse and sustainable financial resources. The chapter underscores the importance of a diverse range of data for measuring community school success beyond traditional academic metrics. The chapter also introduces the logic model as an important tool for planning, evaluation, and communication, explaining how this visual representation can articulate the connection among strategies, activities, and desired outcomes for community schools.

Chapter 6 is an important chapter, but it may be one that more novice community school principals may wish to skim and revisit later in their tenure. It focuses on the principal's vital role in advocating for their community school. This advocacy involves identifying and articulating pressing community needs, building relationships with key stakeholders, and crafting a compelling "elevator pitch" to communicate the value and impact of community schools. This chapter later underscores highlights the power of collective action, encouraging principals to build a broad advocacy team that empowers students, families, community members, and staff to join them in championing community schools.

The book's final chapter explores how community schools can be a powerful tool for achieving a more just educational system. It reinforces the importance of adopting an asset-based approach that both recognizes and leverages the strengths, knowledge, and resources present within the community. This chapter also provides a list of introspective questions that principals can use to maintain an asset-based approach.

❓ Responses from Principals in the Field

At the end of each chapter, I will offer a few questions for readers to consider, answered by a sampling of principals across the country. Much better than I could ever express, these principals explain in their own words how the terms and tenets of this chapter apply to their perspectives and day-to-day experiences.

How do you find the time, and why should you find the time to do this work with all the other demands placed on a principal?

Once schools onboard a community schools coordinator/director and begin the process of strategically aligning resources and reviewing gaps, they are like, "I don't know how we didn't do this before." It just becomes a more efficient way of doing things because it's not all on one person. You're all coming together. You have a collective mindset. It's all hard work. No matter what—education is hard. We're underpaid and overworked for sure. But it's rewarding to have us all in it together rather than feeling like I'm out here on my own trying to figure it out.

Luann Kida, *Executive Director Binghamton University Community Schools, Binghamton, NY*

The needs are always going to be there. But being a community school allows you to surface them and address them. With community schools, you're building out a larger community of people that can respond to the needs of your students and families. In essence, what you're doing is building a bigger tent. Community schools also enable me to delegate, so I don't have to solve all the student-level behavioral problems. I don't have to be the primary instructional leader for every teacher on site. We have other staff that can be assigned to those duties. And as a result, not only does that promote the horizontalism that is really at the core of how we're trying to be together as a site, but it also allows me to get so much more accomplished.

Claudia DeLarios Morán, *Principal Buena Vista/Horace Mann K-8, San Francisco, CA*

A huge part of community schools is taking the time to invest in and build a strong team, because ultimately it means that I can let go and delegate because I know that my team is going to move the school's vision forward, and it's going to get done with high quality. A lot of it is building trust. And once we have built that trust, my team, along with the community school coordinator, are the reasons why I am able to be a more effective leader.

Nicole Jaramillo, *Principal Lavaland Elementary, Albequerque, NM)*

Hopefully, by now you are excited about the prospect of transforming your school into a community school or expanding your school's practices. Before you dive into making that transformation happen, let's gain a deeper understanding of *what* a community school is and ensure we share a common language.

Notes

1 Fernández, A. (2020). *BPS Hub Schools Town Hall*. Boston, MA; National Center for Community Schools. National Center for Community Schools. (2024). *Every school a community school*. Retrieved from https://www.nccs.org
2 Coleman, J. S., Campbell, E. Q., Hobson, C. J., McPartland, J., Mood, A., Weinfeld, F. D., & York, R. L. (1966). *Equality of educational opportunity*.

Washington, DC: US Department of Health, Education, and Welfare, Office of Education.
3. Berliner, D. C. (2009). *Poverty and potential: Out-of-school factors and school success*. Boulder, CO and Tempe, AZ: Education and the Public Interest Center & Education Policy Research Unit. Retrieved from http://files.eric.ed.gov/fulltext/ED507359.pdf
4. Phillips, M., Brooks-Gunn, J., Duncan, G. J., Klebanov, P., & Crane, J. (1998). Family background, parenting practices, and the black-white test score gap. In C. Jencks & M. Phillips (Eds.), *The black-white test score gap* (pp. 103–145). Washington, DC: Brookings Institution Press; see also Rothstein, R. (2010, October 14). *How to fix our schools* (Issue Brief #286). Washington, DC: Economic Policy Institute. Retrieved from www.epi.org/publication/ib286/0
5. Muñoz, M. A., Owens, D., & Bartlett, C. (2015). Removing non-academic barriers in urban schools: School-linked social services. *Planning and Changing, 46*(1/2), 71; Rebell, M. A., Wolff, J. R., & Rogers, J. R., Jr. (2012). *Deficient resources: An analysis of the availability of basic educational resources in high needs schools in eight New York State school districts*. New York, NY: Center for Educational Equity. Retrieved from www.centerforeducationalequity.org/publications/safeguarding-students-educational-rights/DeficientResources.pdf
6. Oakes, J. (2019). Foreword. In J. Ferrara & R. Jacobson (Eds.), *Community schools: People and places transforming education and communities* (pp. ix–xiii). New York, NY: Rowman & Littlefield.
7. See also Anyon, J. (2005). What "counts" as educational policy? Notes toward a new paradigm. *Harvard Educational Review, 75*(1), 65–88; Reville, P. (2020). *The common cause for healthcare and education*. Boston, MA: Center for Primary Care, Harvard Medical School. Retrieved from http://info.primarycare.hms.harvard.edu/blog/common-cause-healthcare-education
8. Kara S. Finnigan, Professor of Educational Policy and Leadership at the University of Rochester spoke of these technical reform strategies at a presentation by the New York Advisory Committee to the U.S. commission on Civil Rights. Finnigan spoke of this technical reform approach as one that views poor educational outcomes as a function of failures within school systems, including but not limited to subpar teaching, weak curriculum, low standards, and too much bureaucracy, among others.

9. Kostyo, S. (2023). *Community school approach reaches high of 60%*. Retrieved from https://fas.org/publication/community-school-approach-reaches-high-of-60-reports-latest-pulse-panel/
10. Maier, A., & Rivera-Rodriguez, A. (2023). *State strategies for investing in community schools*. Palo Alto, CA: Learning Policy Institute.
11. Maryland State Education Association. (n.d.). *Services when and where students need them*. Retrieved from https://marylandeducators.org/community-schools/
12. Schlueb, M. (2024). State funding increase to drive growth in community partnership schools. *UCF Today* (Orlando, FL).
13. Kostyo, S. (2023). *Community school approach reaches high of 60*. Retrieved from https://fas.org/publication/community-school-approach-reaches-high-of-60-reports-latest-pulse-panel/
14. MD S 661. (2019). *Primary and secondary education—Community schools—Established*. Retrieved from https://custom.statenet.com/public/resources.cgi?id=ID:bill:MD2019000S661&ciq=ncsl5&client_md=3a3bd049b324ced05d18381e7aed9811&mode=current_text
15. Oakes, J., Maier, A., & Daniel, J. (2017). *Community schools: An evidence-based strategy for equitable school improvement*. Boulder, CO: National Education Policy Center.
16. Blank, M., Harkavy, I., Quinn, J., Villarreal, L., & Goodman, D. (2023). *The community schools revolution*. Retrieved from https://www.communityschoolsrevolution.org. See specifically: Martinez, L., & Hayes, C. D. (2013). *Measuring social return on investment for community schools: A case study*. Children's Aid Society; Bloodworth, M. R., & Horner, A. C. (2019). *Return on investment of a community school coordinator: A case study*. Retrieved from https://apexeval.org/wp-content/uploads/2022/06/ROI_Coordinator_ABC_2_Column_9.9.19.pdf; Economic Modeling Specialists Inc. (2012). *The economic impact of communities in schools*. Communities in Schools.
17. See Oakes, J., Maier, A., & Daniel, J. (2017). *Community schools: An evidence-based strategy for equitable school improvement*. Boulder, CO: National Education Policy Center, p. 15/16.
18. Campo, S. (2023). *Stages of development*. New York, NY: National Center for Community Schools Children's Aid. Retrieved from https://www.nccs.org/wp-content/uploads/2023/01/CSF_Stages-of-Development-Jan-2023.pdf

19 Composed of partners including the Brookings Institution, the National Center for Community Schools, the Coalition for Community Schools at IEL, and the Learning Policy Institute.
20 Steiner, E. D., Doan, S., Woo, A., Gittens, A. D., Lawrence, R. A., Berdie, L., Wolfe, R. L., Greer, L., & Schwartz, H. L. (2022). *Restoring teacher and principal well-being is an essential step for rebuilding schools.* Retrieved from https://www.rand.org/content/dam/rand/pubs/research_reports/RRA1100/RRA1108-4/RAND_RRA1108-4.pdf
21 Blank, M. J., Berg, A. C., & Melaville, A. (2006). *Growing community schools: The role of cross-boundary leadership.* Coalition for Community Schools. Retrieved from https://www.mikemcmahon.info/community.pdf, p. 3.
22 Blank, M. J., Berg, A. C., & Melaville, A. (2006). *Growing community schools: The role of cross-boundary leadership.* Coalition for Community Schools. Retrieved from https://www.mikemcmahon.info/community.pdf
23 Blank, M. J., Berg, A. C., & Melaville, A. (2006). *Growing community schools: The role of cross-boundary leadership.* Coalition for Community Schools. Retrieved from https://www.mikemcmahon.info/community.pdf, p. 3.
24 Arnold, R. D. & Wade, J. P. (2015). A definition of systems thinking: A systems approach. *Procedia Computer Science, 44,* 669–678.
25 Adapted from the following two sources: Ndaruhutse, S., Jones, C., & Riggall, A. (2019). *Why systems thinking is important for the education sector.* Education Development Trust. Retrieved from https://www.edt.org/research-and-insights/why-systems-thinking-is-important-for-the-education-sector/; Bowman, K., Chettleborough, J., Jeans, H., Whitehead, J., & Rowlands, J. (2015). *Systems thinking: An introduction for Oxfam programme staff.* Retrieved from https://oxfamilibrary.openrepository.com/bitstream/handle/10546/579896/ml-systems-thinking-151020-en.pdf?sequence=1

2

Understanding the "What" and "Why" of Community Schools

Introduction

In 2016, one of our newly elected mayor's initiatives was to start community schools, and I thought, "Yes! This sounds like a great opportunity." But when the complex application process came out, it landed during one of the busiest times of the year, and I remember thinking, "I can't do this. It's too much." But I grabbed my laptop, went to the nurse's office—since she was on long-term leave—and found a quiet space to focus long enough to finish the application. And we were accepted!

We started by hiring a community school coordinator. I interviewed a gentleman who had been volunteering at our school, running a local mentoring group, and living in the community—he was the perfect fit. With him on board, we quickly started building connections. In many ways, we were already operating like a community school, even before the official designation. Partnerships were crucial to our survival as a small elementary school with limited resources. We connected with anyone who could offer support.

However, once we officially became a community school, it became clear we needed to refine our vision. We had to ensure it truly reflected the needs of the students and the community without assuming we knew what those needs were. We conducted a needs assessment, which revealed high levels of food insecurity, mental health challenges, and a lack of recreational spaces outside of school. We developed a vision from these insights and began aligning partnerships with greater intention. It wasn't an overnight transformation, but we started making real progress. With a dedicated team, we were able to offer some unique opportunities for our students. The experience deepened our impact and reinforced the power of collaboration and community.

Chuanika Sanders-Thomas, *former principal of James Logan Elementary, Philadelphia, PA*

DOI: 10.4324/9781032717692-2

For some of you, Principal Sanders' epigraph is rather straightforward and speaks to the power of community schools. For others, there is much to unpack. Either way, principal Sanders underscores much of what this first chapter will be about—namely understanding the "what" and "why" of community schools. There may be some terms that are not familiar, or that people think of in different ways, such as a tool called the needs and assets assessment, the community school coordinator, and collaborative leadership. We will go through all of these terms and ensure we are speaking the same language throughout the book and understand why these strategies and practices are so important.

This chapter will also discuss the evolution of community schools over time—how the community schools of today are far different from the community schools of old—and the importance of distinguishing between the two. Next, this chapter will cover the various contexts that principals may represent, stressing the importance of a context-specific approach. We will also come back to what we touched on in the introduction, specifically, what it means to center systems thinking and the more sophisticated operating system that community schools both require and enable. Finally, we will expose some of the greatest fears inherent in this work. Being a community school principal is heavy responsibility, but one that the many principals I spoke with would vouch for as exponentially worth the risk.

Community Schools: A Common Language

All too often, people hear the term "community schools," but they filter it through their own knowledge and often understand something quite different from one another. This is why it is important to establish a baseline from the start, especially because we are not talking about one single program; rather, a cocktail of strategies that are intentionally integrated.

There are several "short and sweet" definitions of a community school. One of the best I've found is the one mentioned in the introduction:

> Community schools are a strategy that organizes the resources and the voices of the school and community around student success.
>
> (Pat Harvey, former Superintendent of St. Paul Public Schools)

Here are three others:

> Community schools transform traditional public schools into neighborhood hubs that mobilize students, staff, families and community members to reimagine education and co-construct a shared vision for their school and community. (NEA)[1]

> The community schools strategy transforms a school into a place where educators, local community members, families, and students work together to strengthen conditions for student learning and healthy development.
>
> (Learning Policy Impact Brief).[2]

This next definition starts the same way, yet it includes an additional sentence emphasizing the importance of partnerships.

> The community schools strategy transforms a school into a place where educators, local community members, families, and students work together to strengthen conditions for student learning and healthy development. As partners, they organize in- and out-of-school resources, supports, and opportunities so that young people thrive.[3]

Having these broad but pithy definitions in mind can help wrap our heads around what this work is. But what do all these statements mean and look like in practice? What does it look like on the ground?

I'm going to offer three different frameworks to help bring it to life. Perhaps the simplest way to think about community schools in practice is through the four-pillar approach to conceptualizing community schools. Basically, the four-pillar approach is based on a combination of four key features that guide implementation and are intended to yield the transformational outcomes associated with community schools:

1. Expanded and enriched learning time and opportunities: This pillar encompasses academic support and real-world learning opportunities, often during out of school time (i.e. before the start of the school day, afterschool, and during the summer).
2. Collaborative leadership and practices: This pillar focuses on building a shared vision for the work, which includes ongoing professional learning, an emphasis on collective trust, and shared responsibility for outcomes.
3. Active family and community engagement: This pillar involves "actively tapping the expertise and knowledge of family and community members to serve as true partners."[4]
4. Integrated student supports: This pillar references supports and partnerships for academic, physical, social-emotional, and mental health needs, coordinated by a dedicated staff member.

Although some schools and school districts still use the four-pillar framework, many practitioners are shifting away from it to allow more attention to be placed on an integration of the core instructional program. Additionally, practitioners highlight the idea that in a community school, the community itself can be used as a learning resource. There is also a concern that the four-pillar approach may lead to the misconception that each of the pillars can stand alone, without the need for integration or connection.

Realizing some of the limitations of the four-pillar framework, community school leaders across the country[5] banded together to take the best of existing research and resources (including the four pillars) and created an updated framework for what community schools are and can be. Hence, the Community Schools Forward task force was developed in 2023.

This task force arrived at six interconnected key practices. Four are very similar to practices outlined in the four pillars (the titles are slightly different), but they include an instructional component, along with a practice centered on trust and belonging. But the word *interconnected* very well may be the most important piece—as each of these key elements must exist within one carefully developed system. The four pillars are now considered part of six essential practices which include two additional practices:

1. Rigorous, community-connected classroom instruction: Here, teaching and learning focuses on both rigorous content and learning opportunities that connect to students' cultures and the world outside the classroom.
2. A culture of belonging, safety, and care: This practice emphasizes that the school is a welcoming and safe place in which community members can forge trusting relationships.

Again, it is vital to stress that these six key practices are not intended to exist independently. Rather, they are a part of a complex and interconnected whole. Each of these practices supports learning and student development. But it is the synergy among them—along with the enabling conditions such as trust, inclusive decision-making, and a shared vision—that makes the community schools strategy effective.[6]

It is important to note that the Federal Full Service Community Schools program still uses the four-pillar framework; the movement from four pillars to six practices continues to evolve.

A final framework, also developed by the Community Schools Forward Task Force (see Figure 2.1), builds on the six essential practices and illustrates what it means to fully implement a transformational community school.

In order to represent the interconnectedness of the community schools work, the task force created a graphic that is a cross between a jigsaw puzzle and a gear. You'll notice the six key practices just inside the outermost ring, taking up the largest amount of space in the diagram. As you move inward toward the center, you'll next see a set of conditions required to make community schools work, which are the presence of trusting relationships; a shared vision; inclusive decision-making; and actionable data. The next layer toward the center involves the key players in this work, or as the legend shows, those who

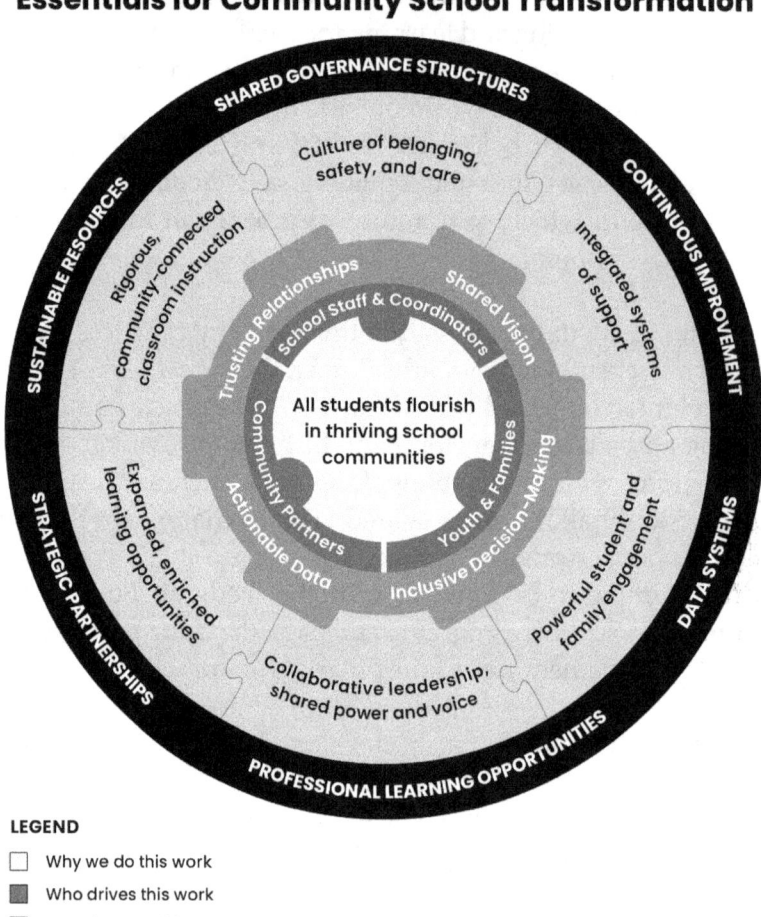

FIGURE 2.1 Community Schools Forward: Essentials for Community School Transformation[8]

drive this work (including community partners, school staff and coordinators, and youth and families). At the very center is the "why" of community schools, the goal being that all students will flourish in thriving school communities. Finally, the outermost dark circle delineates the supportive infrastructure, or systems work, required to make it all run smoothly ... and have staying power. Some of these supports are based within the school, but others can be cultivated and provided by "local, state, and federal policies, ongoing technical assistance, and private and public investments"[7] (p. 4).

Regardless of how community schools are conceptualized, it is critical to note that no two community schools look the same. If they are truly a reflection of local assets and driven by community priorities, they all will look slightly (or very) different. But as the *Community Schools Playbook*, a policy and implementation guide for community schools, explains,

> What [community schools] do share, however, is a commitment to partnership and to rethinking—and at times rebuilding—relationships based on a strong foundation of trust and respect. School staff, under the leadership of the principal and community school director, work with families and community partners to create and implement a shared vision of student and school success.[9]

Now that you have a solid conceptual understanding of community schools, let's get clear on some of the more concrete definitions of what happens in community school practice.

Important Definitions

There are several essential terms that are important to establish at the outset.

Community school coordinator: This term is known in different places as either the community school coordinator (CSC), community school manager (CSM), or the community school director (CSD). I will use the term community school coordinator and the acronym CSC throughout the book, as that was the term that was most widely used by the principals that I interviewed. However, I'm not convinced (and will explain in a moment) that *director* isn't the more apt term.

Nomenclature aside, the coordinator is a full-time high-level resource assigned to one school community whose primary purpose is to identify needs and strengths of the community in order to prime students for learning.

The term "high-level resource" is important here. As a high-level resource, the CSC plays a leadership role, as opposed to the auxiliary staff member who puts out fires or covers lunch duty. This is why the position is often referred to as a community school *director*, versus a coordinator, as it implies that the role is a high-level school administrator, perhaps akin to an assistant principal. The CSC is the person who partners with the principal to identify patterns and develop systems and structures to target those patterns; the CSC is not a direct service provider. For example, they are *not* the person that drives to someone's house to bring the child into school. However, they *are* the person who finds out from numerous families why their students are not coming into school and then develops and manages a system that allows many more families to start getting their children into school. This person also ensures that the work of the partners and community resources is integrated and aligned with the school's instructional program.

It is important to note that not all schools can immediately support a CSC. If that is the case, a school may be able to find an existing staff person who can temporarily assume the community school lens.

But the goal should be that every school has a specifically designated community school coordinator or director who can maintain firm boundaries around their job responsibilities.

Asset-Based Model: Let's now move to a term that is less tactical and more cerebral. In a deficit model, the focus is on what is wrong or lacking. In the context of schools and communities, a deficit approach emphasizes repairing what is broken or addressing gaps. An asset-based model does the opposite. It is focused on the strengths of a group or community, the ones current and in front of our eyes: local residents, existing leaders, informal neighborhood organizations, or local institutions. These assets then become the resources for addressing community needs and priorities, as well as helping to resolve local challenges.

Needs and Assets Assessment: In the more corporate arena, this process is often called a *needs assessment*, a *needs analysis*, or a *gap analysis*. In the world of community schools, this process is often called a Needs and Assets Assessment (and I've also heard it called a "Needs and Opportunities" Assessment). To me, titles that include the words "assets" or "opportunities" feel more in line with the community school ethos and much less deficit-based.

The needs and assets assessment (NAA) generates information specific to the school and its community that guides priority setting and leads to an action plan. Throughout the NAA process, all members of the community, including students, families, and community members, come together to determine community needs, service gaps, and resources that are available to leverage in order to improve student achievement. This process is usually led by the CSC, in concert with the principal.

Collaborative Leadership: In the wise words of Jane Quinn, one of the godmothers of community schools, collaborative leadership "involves sharing decision-making authority between educators and key stakeholders, including parents." Collaborative leadership is about the sharing of power and responsibility—namely the right to make decisions, speak with an equal voice, and be a part of the actual leadership team at the school. This leadership team consists of individuals in the school that assist and advise the principal in decision-making—and this structure typically includes the CSC. Obviously, this works much better when the principals trust and feel full confidence in the teams around them and the teams feel as though they are a valued and integral part of the operation. Why collaborative leadership? Research is strong and persuasive, including studies carried out by the Consortium on Chicago School research,[10] showing that shared leadership is an essential ingredient for school improvement.

We'll dive much deeper into collaborative leadership and the need for a high-performing, high-trust team in Chapter 3.

Different Models of Community Schools: Finally, it is important to point out that there are several different models of community schools, or more specifically, of how the community school coordinator is funded and managed. One such model is often referred to as the **lead agency model**, where an outside, community-based agency leads operations and hires and supervises the CSC. Here, the lead agency acts as both a provider and a broker of services, supports, and opportunities. In other cases, the school or school district assumes this coordinating role and has oversight of operations and the CSC (this is the **district-led model**). There is also a model in which there is a partnership between the school or school district and a local university or college. In this model, **the university-assisted community school**, the university serves as the lead partner and is often in charge of hiring the CSC. Universities can also play a wide range of roles, including a simple one, where students from the university come in and offer tutoring services. School university partnerships can also be really complex; universities can invest in a more visionary approach and truly become a long-term institutional anchor to combat systemic issues.

Importance of a Context-Specific Approach

Knowing that every community school is different, and community schools do and must adapt to their specific contexts, most of this book will still be relevant to a range of different environments—from the most urban to the most rural. But that being said, context does matter. From the 40+ many school leaders I spoke with, every single community had a different set of strengths and assets from which to draw ... and a different set of challenges to contend with. While many of the processes and general strategies presented in this book will be consistent across sites (e.g. the needs and assets assessment process or the role of the community school coordinator), the nuances will always be different. In other words, all work must be carried out in a manner that is responsive to and mindful of place and community.

Please know that as I move through the book, there may be instances where I do not call out contextual differences. However, there will be times when I must point out that a strategy might look different in another context. This is particularly true when regarding an urban or rural environment. However, there is a danger in making sweeping generalizations about either of these contexts—or anything in between or outside them.

Community Schools Then and Now

As mentioned in the introduction, community schools are not a new initiative. Community school historian John Rogers argues that community schools, in one form or another, have existed for over 100 years.[11] He suggests that there have been multiple generations of community schools, with the most recent iteration beginning in the early 1990s. For each of these generations, the goal was to "initiate political change, solve pressing problems, or meet immediate needs."[12]

However, today's community schools often look quite different from those even 30 or so years ago. The short explanation is that there has been a shift from an approach that mostly consisted of providing services for students to a holistic, community-centered approach. Today's community school initiatives put community and community engagement at the forefront in order to get to the root of more systemic issues.

One term used by community schools of old is still occasionally employed today: *wraparound services*. These are services are brought into schools to ensure that needs are met and gaps are filled. Don't get me wrong; there's nothing wrong with making sure that kids' get what they need so that they can focus on academics and succeed in the classroom. But wrap-around services are based on the deficit model, which, when reinforced, limits community schools in what they can do. Adding more and more fragmented services indeed may make temporary

TABLE 2.1 Trends Over 30 Years[13]

Where we were then	Where we are now
♦ Co-location	♦ Collective impact
♦ Adding programs and events	♦ Whole-school transformation
♦ CBOs as vendors	♦ CBOS as partners
♦ Wrap around services (often about "fixing" kids)	♦ Integrated services, opportunities, and supports
♦ Program-centered	♦ Student-centered
♦ Time-limited project	♦ Long-term strategy
♦ Innovators developing one or a few schools	♦ Developing systems of community schools
♦ Targeted on struggling schools	♦ The way we do school

improvements in school and community life. But the changes will not be transformational, meaning the root issues will remain immutable. Even with the addition of essential high-quality programs, everything needs to be part of a connected system of support, and part of a system in which (in the words we heard earlier from Patricia Harvey) community voices and resources are organized around student success.

Abe Fernández, director of the National Center for Community Schools, gives an amazing Community Schools 101 presentation that I will try to replicate here (see Table 2.1).

One element of Abe's presentation involves the naming of some trends that have evolved over the course of the past few decades. One indicates a shift from a perspective on partners as service-providers who are co-located in schools, or have space within schools to do their work, to a system that sees partners as more than service providers. In fact, partners are seen as integral parts of a collective-impact approach; they are co-planners who share accountability for results.

Abe also underlines a shift away from being program-centered. He and others sometimes refer to this as the Christmas Tree model—where it's all about new shiny ornaments (programs) that are plentiful and pretty, but not intentional or organized in any specific way. They are also not centered around what students truly need or what communities prioritize.

Community schools are also not a quick fix. They are a long-term strategy, focused on more than just adding programs or changing one element of school life. Community schools of today are not just for the most struggling schools or for the most struggling students, but they require us all to think differently about what schools mean for their students and their communities—in other words—"the way we do school."[14]

Fears of Being a Community School Principal

In my conversations with principals, they made it clear that taking on this kind of leadership role meant confronting some fears. Being a principal itself is scary. The responsibility—the risk—and the weight of your decisions and choices are enormous. Research says that the principal's role, along with that of the teacher, is one of the two most important school-related factors that impact student achievement.[15] That's a hefty responsibility.

There is so much accountability that rests on the shoulders of principals, some coming down from district leadership, and some that emanates from the families and the community. Districts also want to make sure their leaders are "performing" and that results are improving immediately. The fear of being reassigned is real. There is a reason that principal turnover is so rampant.

Being a community school principal adds yet another layer of fear or risk. There's a fear that what you're doing, what you believe in so deeply, is not actually going to make a difference. There is a fear that it will make a difference, but the results will not show in a way that would be tangible for the community and the district at large. There is also a fear that the changes will not happen quickly enough. There are many other fears too. What happens if the funding runs out? How am I going to manage my new staff members? What happens if I see the data emerging from the community—and it is soul crushing?

But the day-to-day challenges that you face as a principal are always going to be there, whether you are a community school or not.

And real, meaningful change takes time. As Principal Mark Gaither explained,

> Like so many things in this world, we look at a problem or situation we find ourselves in and we want a solution—we demand a solution from the people working on it—in a matter of days, weeks, months, or years. But when we look at it, the situation itself has developed over years or decades. We hope for a simple solution, but the reality is that we need a sophisticated solution, something that can fundamentally address the issue versus a solution that gives immediate results but doesn't solve the problem.
>
> **Mark Gaither**, *current Principal of Wolfe Street Academy, Baltimore, MD*

Issues facing students, families, and communities are deeply entrenched and multigenerational. Outcomes will not change overnight, even with a sophisticated and data-backed solution such as community schools.

As I mentioned in the introduction, there are many principals out there who are doing much, if not all, of this already, even if their schools are not designated community schools. Many already have a community-oriented lens and are out there, pounding the pavement, looking for community assets in different forms, leveraging them in many different ways, and even fully immersing them into school life. There are principals who already think deeply about the whole child, working to ensure that every student has the support and experiences to thrive. There are principals who have made impressive inroads around authentic parent engagement. They are uniters; collaborative leaders, who bring teachers, staff, parents/guardians; and community members around a collective vision. There are those who have taken many, many risks along the way.

And whether it's shifting your practice and incorporating more community school strategies, building on some of the community school-oriented strategies that are already in place, or even starting completely from scratch, community schools can feel like a daunting proposition. But know that there are so many others across the country that have, and are, taking these steps as a leap of faith. And this book, along with practitioners and leaders far and wide, is here to support you along every step of the journey.

(?) Responses from Principals in the Field

As promised in the introduction, this chapter concludes by featuring the voices of principals answering one targeted question.

What would you say that your community school does that differentiates it from a more traditional school?

The more traditional model leans toward "We're the school and you're the families. We tell you what we need and you make it happen." With the community school, it's more interconnected. Everybody works to understand everybody's needs. We're not just going to say "Your child needs to do better in school." "We're going to find out the root causes for any deficiencies and then figure out how we can work together to address them. It's no longer an "us versus them." It has to be "we." Community schools are a conduit to get those conversations going and build that understanding. And then my role as principal is to be the bridge.

Jo-Anne Knapp, *former Principal of Caryl E. Adams Elementary School, Whitney Point, NY*

Prior to becoming a community school principal, I would be at one meeting talking about a problem and at another meeting talking about the same problem, and it would the same kid we're talking about, but it would be different groups of people trying to solve the problem—which made no sense. When we became a community school, we created systems to coordinate and align around how we're talking about kids and the ways in which we want to support them. And we started using a more assets-based lens because these conversations often went down to the blaming of this and the blaming of that. We needed a shift in our thinking, including realizing that we're not a bunch of different teams all doing different things. We're one team and we're all working together. It was through this community school work that we were able to get to that point.

Ann Hanna, *Community School Consultant in the Maine Department of Education and Former Principal at Gerald E. Talbot Community School, Portland, ME*

—

Traditionally, schools are set in communities where the school's job is to "certify" their kids. ABCDs, suspensions, you're a kid who will go to college, you're a kid who will go to trade school, etc. That's traditionally the role of school. They're like an outside agency, inside of a community, that is certifying children. Community schools flip this narrative. The school is situated inside a community, and so it becomes a resource for that community. But community schools are not just about partnerships, and the fact that you have thousands of partnerships does not make you a community school. What makes you a community school, at the core, is the needs and assets assessment process, compiled in tandem with students, caregivers, families, educators, and the organizations that you feel that are part of your community. This is not data generated from the district like absenteeism, suspension rates, D's and F's. This is data based upon needs and experiences of the various entities. For organizations, it might be that they are wanting to have access to students or educators, or it could be space at the school. For educators, it might be that they need more resources—or they don't have enough time to collaborate or call families. So when you do the needs and assets assessment, the decision-making body that is tasked with making heads or tails of it then makes carefully informed decisions and develops strategic partnerships based upon the needs.

> **Michael Essien**, *former Principal of Martin Luther King Jr. Academic Middle School, San Francisco, CA and current Director of Community Schools and Partnerships for Alameda County Office of Education*

In a traditional school, the accountability that we have had, up to now, comes from the outside. It is imposed onto a school. If a school is underperforming, either you close it, or you restructure it, or you give it to an agency to handle. And this has happened in multiple districts. Community schools are based on the development of what I like to call "relational accountability," which is all about trust with your own teachers and with your own community. It's about the intersection of what happens inside the school and what is connected outside. When you start to take a closer look at issues that affect family, life, and the community, people begin to trust us. They say, "You care about me, my children, and my families," and when you do that, then their resistance to be engaged inside the school decreases because they know you mean the best. In community schools, we look at the trilogy of school quality, family engagement, and community engagement. With community schools, you finally have the right formula to advance achievement.

> **Carlos Azcoitia**, *former Principal at John Spry Community School and Community Links High School (a prek-12 model), Chicago, IL*

Now that we have established some of the foundational concepts of community schools, the next chapter will examine how to create a shared vision and foster collaborative leadership to guide the work of becoming a community school.

Notes

1. National Education Association. (2024). *Meeting the needs of students with community schools.* Retrieved from https://www.nea.org/student-success/great-public-schools/community-schools?utm_medium=paid-search&utm_source=google&utm_campaign=community-schools&utm_content=&ms=ads-community-schools-se&gad_source=1&gclid=eaiaiqobchmihyjin-3jhqmv12hhar2xewdjeaayasaaegitdvd_bwe&gclsrc=aw.ds
2. Burns, D., Griffith, M., Maier, A. (2023). *Funding community schools in California.* Retrieved from https://learningpolicyinstitute.org/product/funding-community-schools-california-brief.
3. New York State Community Schools Network. (2024). Retrieved from https://www.nyscsn.org
4. State Transformational Assistance Center for Community Schools. (2022). California Department of Education. Retrieved from https://scs.gseis.ucla.edu/resources/project-example-3-grey/
5. These four partners are Children's Aid National Center for Community Schools (NCCS), Center for Universal Education at the Brookings Institution, the Coalition for Community Schools at the Institute for Educational Learning (IEL), and the Learning Policy Institute (LPI).
6. Wise words of Abe Fernández, Director of the National Center for Community Schools.
7. Community schools forward. (2023). *Framework: Essentials for community school transformation.* Retrieved from https://learningpolicyinstitute.org/project/community-schools-forward
8. Community Schools Forward. (2023). *Framework: Essentials for community school transformation.* Retrieved from https://learningpolicyinstitute.org/project/community-schools-forward
9. Partnership for the Future of Learning. (n.d.). *Community schools playbook.* Retrieved from https://communityschools.futureforlearning.org/assets/downloads/community-schools-playbook.pdf
10. Sebring, P. B., & Bryk, A. S. (2000). School leadership and the bottom line in Chicago. *Phi Delta Kappan, 81*(6), 440–443.
11. Rogers, J. S. (1998). Community schools: Lessons from the past and present. *Unpublished manuscript,* 133–174.
12. Rogers, J. S. (1998). Community schools: Lessons from the past and present. *Unpublished manuscript,* 133–174, p. 16.

13. Fernández, A. (2020). *BPS Hub Schools Town Hall*. Boston, MA; National Center for Community Schools. Please note that Abe Fernández is Director of National Center for Community Schools at Children's Aid.
14. McLaughlin, M., Fehrer, K., & Leos-Urbel, J. (2020). *The way we do school: The making of Oakland's full-service community school district*. Cambridge, MA: Harvard Education Press.
15. Leithwood, K., Seashore, K., Anderson, S., & Wahlstrom, K. (2004). *Review of research: How leadership influences student learning*. Retrieved from https://wallacefoundation.org/sites/default/files/2023-07/How-Leadership-Influences-Student-Learning.pdf

3

Creating a State of Readiness

Introduction

This chapter focuses on creating a state of readiness to take on "the work" of being a community school by developing a vision for your school's intended future. If you are already an emerging or well-established community school, these concepts will still apply and can be reference points for reinforcing and building on what is already in place.

Because community schools are not a formulaic approach to how you do school, rather a set of interconnected strategies, you will find that there are many possible ways to start. I suggest in this chapter that the work begins with the *vision*. But there is also a sound argument for initiating the work with a needs and assets assessment, or even by making sure that the principal has a community school coordinator or someone who can assume this function from the get-go. As my colleague Jane Quinn shared, there are many metaphors that apply to launching or growing a community school: there are many doors, many right answers, and many different potential on-ramps.

The no-brainer about readiness for community schools is what we talked about in the introduction and the first chapter: first, there must be an understanding of what it means to be a community school, both in terms of what being a community school is and what it isn't. The school leader must also have the language to articulate this understanding to their school community. Some soul-searching may need to take place for this. Recall that being a part of a community school means both operating through an asset-based lens and being a systems-thinker—more importantly, a systems thinker that is constantly looking to improve and refresh systems that are currently in place. Are you, as a school leader, really there? Whether you are building on existing community school practices or starting anew, is there a willingness to shift and improve the way you "do" business? Is there a recognition that the work ahead may result in significant changes to the status quo, including changes in roles and responsibilities? All of these mindset qualities must first and foremost be understood by the school leader so they can be shared and embodied by the entire school community. Then, the question becomes "where do we start the work?"

When pressed, the principals that I spoke with about becoming or increasing the capacity of a community school mentioned one word over and over: "vision." In order to set the stage for the work ahead, they believe you start by creating a vision with the school community that is aligned with the values and direction of the school. So, what is this idea of vision and how does it play out in community schools? How do principals take the concrete steps to develop a vision, get the community on the same page, and prepare for its implementation? This chapter will explore the meaning of vision by examining its various forms and levels, followed by a discussion on cultivating collaborative leadership structures in order to achieve it.

Vision 101

Let's start by isolating the idea of vision. A common assumption is that for changes to the status quo to occur in any organization or school context, there needs to be a clear vision of what one is hoping to accomplish. That is as true for a school taking on a new math program as it is for a school wanting to make bigger and bolder changes. Vision, *really* simply put, is:

The combination of a direction or a goal and a plan for how it's going to get accomplished.

There is one more important component of vision: the power to motivate and inspire.[1] A vision is designed to guide behavior, and it involves a rallying aspect, a means of engaging a group of humans to work together to achieve a goal. Here, you might be wondering what the difference is between a vision and a mission statement. While there are organizations that use the two terms interchangeably, a mission statement defines an organization's overall purpose, and the vision defines where the organization aims to go in the future. Often, vision statements, especially in a school context, end up as a combination of the two.[2]

We just defined the term vision as a goal and a means of accomplishing it, coupled with some inspiration to get onboard. So how does a school leader guide and develop this vision? Principals pursue vision development work in one of three different ways. First, they can create a vision for the school and then foist it on others in the community. Even if this vision is amazing and inspirational, we can all see the inherent problems here. People generally will not hop on someone else's bandwagon unless they see the end game and feel as though there is a good reason to pursue that goal.

According to Bert Nanus, author of *Visionary Leadership*, "A vision is little more than an empty dream until it is widely shared and accepted."[3] That suggests there are two other ways that a vision can be offered to a community. The first is a **personal vision that is widely shared and accepted** (even if not developed collaboratively). The second is a **vision borne of collaboration**.

While it may seem obvious that a collaboratively developed vision is the unadulterated winner of the "best kind of vision" contest, the truth is that it's a bit more nuanced. With a "ready-made" or "predesigned" vision, you gain the gift of speed. A school leader has the ability to take the vision and run with it immediately. Also, fewer inputs (i.e. a smaller and simpler process) may result in a more clear and more cohesive articulation of the vision. However, the negatives are obvious. With a predesigned vision, you risk resistance and a lack of community buy-in. Taking the time to invest in codeveloping a vision often leads to a greater likelihood of shared ownership and acceptance. In other words, those around you will likely have more proverbial skin in the game. A shared vision also helps ensure that the vision endures, even though there may be a change in leadership. But because this process is labor intensive and not a quick fix, it is possible that you lose the ability to respond to urgent or immediate needs.

So how did principals I interviewed weigh in on how to get to a shared vision? Was it more the approach of having a ready-made vision (inherited or newly crafted) or did they go through a more comprehensive process of getting community buy-in? Not surprisingly, school leaders discussed a wide range of approaches, often combining multiple strategies. Let's look more closely at the journey of Claudia DeLarios Morán (Buena Vista/Horace Mann K-8, San Francisco, CA), who initiated visioning process from the ground up. She designed an activity for school staff using dot stickers and then involving the broader school community in a development and revision process centered on values.

> Early on we created a vision in our school where we took our staff through a process where they identified the values that are most important to them through sort of a dot-voting, "dotmocracy" process (there were a bunch of different values and everybody was given a number of stickers). So they basically voted on what were their most important values, what was their number one choice, their second choice, and third, and then we asked for volunteers to form a working group. This group then turned those values into the first draft of a statement that they took back to the staff. Then the staff workshopped it together in small groups, and other drafts came out of it. The working group then refined it, refined it, and refined it again until we were all good with the vision as it stood.

Principal Delarios-Morán went on to stress the importance of some of the more human elements of the process, especially when it came to the school culture and sense of belonging.

I need to say that I don't think you can talk about the vision and expect people to sign on to something bigger than themselves if they don't feel like their needs are being met. People need to feel seen. But then you don't want to stay in that place of self-centeredness—you want to move them into a larger understanding of what we're all here to do. So I think that especially if you're a new principal, a new person to the community, you want to lead with that. In a perfect world, the whole first year should be about getting to know the school, the culture, the people, the students, and families. What is it that people need in order to feel like part of something bigger? And then we start talking about what we think the vision is, if there is not already a vision. What do we stand for, all of us? What do we have commonality about? What can we make common cause around? You don't always have to wait till the end of the first year to start having those conversations about the vision, but you need to be noticing things and reflecting them back and asking questions. Do you like it? Should we do something about it? Is this who we want to be? I think it's a way of showing your staff that you're paying attention, you see them, you care, you know, and that also you're here to take it to another level, to contribute in a way to a level of organization that hadn't existed otherwise.

The process at the Buena Vista/Horace Mann school is certainly one that falls into the category of involving numerous stakeholders. Delarios-Morán's statement also shows how she valued the existing culture of the school and the needs of all the individuals involved. That level of awareness is a critical precursor for crafting a vision statement.[4]

Regardless of the overall process, it is important to start with a clear picture and deep understanding of the organization, your school, and your staff, gathering as much information as possible about the way your school ecosystem functions at that very moment and examining what is already in place. What are the current systems, attitudes, beliefs within your school, within your school district, and in relation to the community around it? What is the school's current raison d'étre? It is also helpful to look beyond the school walls. What is the current perception of the school as it stands right now? Are families excited to send their students to this school? What do different community members think about this school? What is expected of the school from different constituencies?

With this knowledge in hand, the principal can then get the right people and voices at the table either to begin the brainstorming process or consider sharing a previously crafted vision. These people may include parents, students, and members of the broader community. To corral their ideas into creating a vision, researchers have recommended a two-step process.[5]

Step One: The first step is for the school principal to give each member of those included in the planning process a series of open-ended questions such as:

What is unique about this school?
What is the current approach and can it be defended? Is it the right approach for the school right now?[6]
What will be different about this school three years from now?
What are the strengths of the school? What are its weaknesses?

Step Two: The second step is for each member to respond to the questions in writing *before* they even come together for the planning session. When they do convene, each member shares their responses and looks for areas of consensus. For the areas in which there is no or limited consensus, the first step is to figure out where there is common ground. Then, the group can draft a statement based on these shared agreements. However, it is important to remember that consensus is really just a lack of serious dissent. In fact, there is not always 100% agreement. As the late researcher Joseph Rogus reminds us, "Not everyone needs to be wildly enthusiastic about an idea for it to be included in the final statement."[7]

A visual gesture tool such as "fist to five" can be a simple but useful mechanism to gage and then work toward consensus. With fist to five, group members demonstrate their input on a range of issues by raising their hand and presenting a number of fingers or a closed fist according to their level of support.

The finger/fist scale is as follows:

A closed fist: This signals complete opposition and desire to block the idea.
One finger: This signals major issues that need to be resolved immediately.
Two fingers: This signals minor issues that need to be resolved immediately.
Three fingers: This signals minor issues that can be resolved at a later time.
Four fingers: This signals full agreement as is.
Five fingers: This signals full agreement and future championing.

Once the group has a series of statements that have achieved consensus, a vision statement is then drafted, and the group then provides a final set of comments. Comments are then considered, changes may be made, and then the vision statement goes to the entire staff for approval. At that point, the document is ready for translation into relevant languages and distribution.

After the vision statement is committed to paper, Rogus continues, it cannot just "sit" there. It must be periodically revisited, perhaps prior to the start of every new school year.[8] At whatever interval makes sense, the school faculty should examine each separate component of the vision and determine 1) whether each part continues to be a critical focus and 2) to what extent the school is making progress in that area. If an area determined to be a critical focus is not being fully realized, that element can be a priority or focus for the following year.

It is also important to add that an essential tool for helping to determine the vision is the *needs and assets assessment* that we will explore in the next chapter. If the school has conducted such assessments in the past, they can and should be used to inform the process. Often, the assets and needs assessment happens later, once the vision is established and collaborative leadership structures are put in place. Such visioning sets the stage for the needs and assets process as well as the planning process that emerges, both of which will be discussed in Chapter 4. Here, it is important to *really* underscore that these interrelated strategies can happen in many different orders. While I have found a way to speak about them in a linear fashion, truly, all the parts are so interrelated that they can happen in myriad orders. In fact, some may happen at the same time. Regardless of sequence, the end goal is the same: the vision becomes the north star guiding the decisions and processes for the school.

Vision as North Star

Once the vision is finalized, the work of developing a culture in which the vision becomes the north star for the whole school staff begins. In a perfect world, each member of the school community knows the vision, believes in the vision, is committed to realizing the vision, and knows their own specific role in achieving the vision. A favorite tool to make that happen is the broken-record approach.

Broken Record Approach

Simply put, with this approach, the vision is repeated until it becomes impossible to ignore. The principal is the orchestrator of this relentless quest to keep the vision at the forefront. They are responsible for reminding the community about the vision (over and over again) and for persistently tying all decision-making processes to the realization of the vision. The principal is also trying to rally their colleagues to talk about the vision whenever relevant and possible.[9] So yes, it's a broken record, but it's also marketing—it's marketing the vision as the north star, worthy of being fully embedded into the culture of the school.

At PW Moore Elementary School in Elizabeth City, NC, Principal Stephanie Ambrose has a weekly newsletter that keeps the vision at the forefront. Another principal spoke about making sure that the vision lives on the bottom of all of school documents and on the agendas for all of governance meetings. Yet another school leader shared that all professional development was linked to the vision, and any associated documents would be aligned with the vision.

Finally, when trying to center and uplift the vision, principals highlighted the human skills of being accessible and communicating openly as key.

As one principal explained,

> On the one hand, you need to be able to articulate that vision. But you also must be responsive and accessible. If there's a question, you need to be available to provide that clarity, rather than, "Oh, I didn't catch him today or maybe I'll get him next week." I was someone who was not only accessible, but I also was big on regular communication and contact. It doesn't have to be an hour-long meeting, but we do need those regular touch points just so that we are constantly calibrating and being responsive to the things that are happening within the school.

Appendix B provides an example of a school vision and the school's path to creating that vision.

A Community of Practice

How *does* everyone within the school community fit into this common vision? How do you ensure that everyone has a piece of ownership, or skin in the game, if you will? One principal even mentioned that *all* members of the community must be tapped, "from bus drivers to educators." Principal Queena Kim (UCLA K-12 Community School in, Los Angeles CA) shared her approach:

> We came together as a staff and were able to formulate what the vision meant to each one of us. What does it mean to me as a teacher? What does it mean at every level? It's not just looking at the roles and responsibilities, but it's looking at the roles and responsibilities in relation to the school's vision. Everyone needs to see that they have a stake in the work, a commitment to the

school, but they also have a responsibility to contribute in pursuit of this vision.

One of the major questions that Principal Kim raises is: What are the different roles, and how do they fit together? People often focus solely on the community school coordinator (defined in Chapter 2 and deeply explored in Chapter 4), but every staff member has a role to play. How do they come together around realizing the vision? Systems thinking and structures are important, but this concept of human buy-in and knowing each person's discrete role moves the work from what several principals described as the transactional to the transformational.

Building a community of practice involves getting the staff members on the same page and creating a school-wide community of practice that includes every single human in the ecosystem. This cannot happen without collaborative leadership structures.

Collaborative Leadership

Collaborative leadership—also called shared leadership, distributive leadership, or democratic leadership—is a core tenet of community schools. It is a leadership style that emphasizes the entire team or community's participation and input in strategic planning, decision-making, and implementation. Collaborative leadership recognizes that schools must have multiple leaders, both within and outside of the administration. In fact, when some researchers study collaborative leadership, their unit of analysis is not the leader. In other words, they are not studying leaders, rather they are studying the leadership practices themselves.[10] With collaborative leadership, leaders no longer operate as "lone wolves." They broaden their wolf packs and are stronger for it.

Whatever your metaphor or what you choose to call it, collaborative leadership is not a simple proposition. In many cases, the proverbial buck stops with the principal. For example, when the data coming out of the school is not trending in the right direction or an incident happens on campus and the principal is then seen as having insufficient management skills, their job is often on the line. When the principal is constantly feeling the weight of the entire school (and sometimes community) on their shoulders, collaborative leadership and allowing others to be part of the decision-making processes might feel counterintuitive. As we discussed in Chapter 2, the evidence that supports collaborative leadership is strong. In fact, research has found that in productive schools, principals "look for opportunities to bring parents, teachers, and other staff into leadership positions, because they know that change requires the commitment, talent, and energy of many."[11]

So how do you get to collaborative leadership, a practice so central to the thriving of community schools? The shared vision is a good place to start. If all members of the school staff are deeply invested in achieving the school vision, then leadership structures and systems can shift accordingly. These structures and systems become grounded in the shared vision, and all members of the community start to think differently about the work.

Claudia DeLarios Morán, who shared her journey to creating a vision earlier in the chapter, has an important perspective on how a shared leadership model engage the school community in the process of realizing the school vision.

> I honestly don't think that we could uphold our vision if we didn't have a shared leadership model. If you're going to ask adults for this level of buy-in, as opposed to just showing up and being the seventh-grade English teacher, they are going to want to be seen and heard as decision-makers and fully fledged members of the community, not just a cog in the wheel. And so the question becomes, how are we giving them agency in the decision-making process?
>
> There are a couple of ways we do that. Every week, each grade-level team meets for an extended period of time.

They're actually released from their teaching obligations, and the kids are with enrichment providers. During this time, the team is meeting together to reflect on a project that they've done in the last week or so, to plan for upcoming projects, or to coordinate their plans as a grade-level team. That could be a field trip or about something coming up around social emotional needs. You know, our first-grade kids are really struggling to keep their hands to themselves. Let's pull the first-grade counselor into this conversation and figure out how we can have a consistent dialogue that every child, regardless of what class they're in, is going to benefit from. So those conversations happen during that protected time.

There is going to be a range in which principals fit along a continuum that runs from non-collaborative to collaborative leadership. One helpful metaphor that illustrates the two different ends of this continuum is the idea of leader as *hero* and leader as *host*, phrases coined by Margaret Wheatley and Debbie Frieze.[12] The leader-as-hero, not surprisingly, exerts high levels of control and has (or is expected to have) all the answers. The assumption is that with strong and clear directives from the leader, school staff will fall in line.

In contrast, leaders-as-hosts prioritize bringing together different members of the community to approach challenges and create opportunities in new and innovative ways. They recognize that many members of the community can be trusted to go beyond their roles on the organizational chart, becoming valuable thought partners and decision-makers, and they are willing to invest in this approach. Leaders-as-hosts trust that all adults can be leaders and take on leadership roles. They also recognize when to step aside and allow others to lead. Wheatley and Frieze talk about this continuum as a journey, where many leaders evolve from leaders-as-heroes to leaders-as-hosts.

It is important to note that the principal cannot just anoint oneself as leader-as-host and foster a productive system of collaborative leadership unless the human elements are established through an ongoing emphasis on relationship building and the cultivation of a culture of trust that enables collaborative decision-making to take place. But leaders-as-hosts don't just trust that ceding control and bringing others into the leadership fold will yield the intended results. Leaders-as-hosts must work hard to foster collaborative leadership. They also must have an understanding that collaborative leadership can be messy and uncomfortable, and some mistakes will be made by all parties involved.

Wheatley and Frieze present a series of strategic and conceptual skills that leaders-as-hosts must develop and put into practice[13]:

1. Know that time is the "scarcest commodity of all," and thereby carve out time and space for collaboration.
2. Provide structures that enable groups of people to work together and allow for different types of leadership roles and different types of coaching and mentoring.
3. Reduce unnecessary paperwork and "administrivia," instead work with people and teams to "develop relevant measures of progress to make their achievements visible."

Carving out sacred time to meet and streamlining "administrivia" are important components, but it's #2 that articulates the importance of cross-sector partnerships at the systems level, which require thinking through the way the school does business every day.

Amy Nerich, principal of the Ford Elementary School in Lynn, MA described how she approaches these elements at her school:

> Providing opportunities for collaboration is critical for successful teachers, successful students, and successful schools. This intentional time for staff partnership allows for staff members to reflect on and analyze practices that are already in existence. As principals, it

is our responsibility to schedule collaboration time and ensure that it is kept sacred. In other words, it should never be canceled or repurposed for a different agenda. If school communities see that collaboration time is a priority in the eyes of the building leaders, they too will take it seriously. At the Ford, staff members are active participants in the collaboration process. Roles are assigned for each meeting, agendas are generated collaboratively and in advance, and at the end of every meeting, the group accounts for next steps. In an ideal situation, staff members will gain the agency to structure and facilitate collaboration time without representatives from administration present—this is the ultimate goal.

The human leadership skills that both principals and researchers noted must also be honed:

1. Model and insist that community members will both make mistakes and learn from the experience, sometimes repeatedly.[14]
2. Local perspectives must be heard and honored.
3. Show your support in such a way that people know the leader has their back.[15]
4. Regularly communicate how your teams and individuals are making progress and what they've accomplished, especially in relation to where they started.[16]
5. "Value conviviality and esprit de corps- not false rah-rah activities, but the spirit that arises in any group that accomplishes difficult work together" (p. 3).[17]

With all this background in mind, the principal's job is to think through the different teams that need to meet and build the systems and structures that enable and facilitate that teamwork. Examples may include professional learning communities, grade-level or site-based teams, teacher-led professional development sessions, peer classroom visits, instructional leadership teams, and core leadership teams.

Dr. Mary White (Principal of North Salinas High School, Salinas, CA) talks about how her superintendent celebrated her practice of building a web of "mini principals," who are not just teachers, but different school staff members. As she explained,

> My job is not to micromanage my staff. My whole school team, including secretaries and our clerical staff, needs to be honored by being allowed to do their jobs fully. My superintendent, whom I've known for years, said to me, "Mary, you just build all these little mini principals throughout your whole school." I said "Well, that's how you get everything done." Because in my first three years. I was just in a state of exhaustion every day because I had to build the capacity. Now I have people who want to do it. They don't need me, and it's joyous. So we've got all these systems operating without my voice having to be at the center.

Mark Gaither, principal of Wolfe Street Academy in Baltimore Maryland, shared his journey from leader-as-hero to leader-as-host.

> I think in the beginning of my principalship, which is also the beginning of my time as a community school principal, I did a lot on my own, or I was really just the connection vehicle between different people. That's a far cry from the structures I have now where I bring together all the different people who can help me make decisions and all the people who make up the different parts of the school governance (special education, after-school, academics ESOL, etc.). They each bring a perspective and strong opinion, and they serve as my most trusted advisors.

Principal Gaither also has a core leadership team that meets weekly. He calls it his "Team of Rivals," a reference to Doris Kearns Goodwin's book that described Abe Lincoln's path to recruiting some of his greatest rivals to serve on his presidential cabinet. Gaither intentionally includes diverse perspectives in his most critical decision-making processes to avoid complacency and ensure continuous feedback on his systems and culture.

Jennifer Stefan, principal of King Elementary in Deer River, MN, talks specifically about getting her staff on the same page and the collaborative leadership structures that she has in place.

> In order to get people rowing in the right direction, you have to have a vision, and you have to communicate that vision to your staff. We have a leadership team, both at the elementary and the high school, and we have weekly professional development. Anytime we needed to talk about instruction or community schools, we have that avenue to be able to do that with staff. So it's not like I have to have a separate staff meeting to get people on the same page and to get them working collaboratively. That system is in place for common planning time for teachers, and then our early-out [dismissal] structure is huge. Our leadership is teacher leaders. That's a critical piece. It's both our teacher leaders and then administrative leaders who put that in place. We've had early-out PLC structure since I became principal. Our common planning time was in place, but it is my job to make that a priority.

At Lavaland Elementary in Albequerque, NM, their school vision is *actually* referred to as Lavaland's north star. Their principal, Nicole Jaramillo, has created teams and leadership opportunities based on three of the key strategies laid out in their vision. As their project-based learning specialist explained,

> Our principal announced to the school that we were creating these teams. And if you'd like to lead, you actually have to give an elevator pitch to the school about why you should be leading this team. Then, the school staff

voted on who they would want to be their leadership representative. Once the leadership was picked, everybody from each grade level was distributed amongst the leadership team so that it wasn't not just one grade level making those decisions.

Principal Jaramillo shared more.

The people that are really passionate about the work are the ones that became the leaders of those teams and now comprise our instructional Council. I really believe in making sure that we are maximizing the knowledge and expertise of the teachers on campus rather than bringing people from outside. Not only is that expensive, but there's not a lot of investment and buy in because the teachers are like, "Who's this person to tell us what to do?" The teachers that are leading our teams have been here for several years and have relational capacity with staff. They are well liked, and they're well trusted. And those are the reasons we've been able to gain so much traction with the work that we're doing over the past several years.

Undergoing a democratic process that prioritizes internal expertise and a foundation of trust can be a means of getting different leaders to assume different leadership roles. Another way that principals can approach how they get new leaders to the table is by a power mapping exercise.[18] These can be more formal, or they can consist of questions such as:

- Who has the power to influence systems within the school (keeping in mind that these individuals may have a loud presence or wield their power more discreetly)?
- How can these individuals be leveraged in order to make the changes necessary to support the community schools work and progress toward achieving the vision?

Finally, and moving from big picture to very micro, Pat Follette, former Superintendent of Whitney Point, NY schools, shared a small but important place to start. She called out the language used to create a culture of collaborative leadership. As she offered,

> Because community schools are a very collaborative and inclusive venture, instead of saying "my community school," I started to say "our" or the "district's community school." Using "me" or "my" is the antithesis of what we're working for. Whenever I worked with or talked about teachers, I would not say "my teachers"; I always said "the teachers I'm working with." With families, they're not "my families." They're the families with children who attend or are part of our school community. Changing to a collaborative, inclusive language is essential in community school work. Another example is that it's not "the principal's initiative." It belongs to the school, and it belongs to the community.

While language is only one small step, this subtle shift inherently creates a culture in which others need to be brought into the fold. A proverb often referenced in my interviews with principals is this:

> If you want to go fast, go alone. If you want to go further, go together.

Working as a team may be slower, but ultimately it will get you farther than you could ever imagine. In a community school context, harnessing the collective wisdom of all stakeholders in order to achieve the vision and believing that everyone has skin in the game and can take ownership of different elements of the work ahead will yield the most powerful results.

This chapter, as those that came before it, concludes with responses from principals in the field.

❓ Responses from Principals in the Field

How did you get past the lone wolf stage of leadership to begin to trust and delegate?

There was definitely a lone wolf time for me. But now, looking back, I would recast the notion of the lone wolf stage to a developmental phase. This phase would involve extensive listening, observing, recording, dissecting and then piecing together all of this data, some qualitative and some quantitative.

For me, it was out of necessity. I knew I needed to get past the lone wolf stage in order to have a life outside of school and keep myself from burning out. I knew that I needed the people around me to help carry the weight, because it is heavy, and there is a lot to be done. I wasn't shy about expressing that I find people around me much smarter than I am. I was and am the first person to say that. When I observe my teachers, I am always looking for teachers who crave more—who have sparks. What can that teacher bring? I need to assemble a team to get to the vision I want. Bringing more people to the table lessens the load from the leader and distributes that ownership to a bigger coalition.

Anthony Frye, *Principal at the Washington S.T.E.M. Elementary School, Lynn, MA*

The "lone wolf stage" requires self-introspection. During this time, you develop and share a plan of action for reaching out and engaging supporters and advocates. You think through all the actions needed to enable faculty and staff members to interact and to share knowledge and relevant experiences with those from a variety of backgrounds. These carefully planned and well executed "cross boundary engagements" are what's likely to build the momentum for establishing viable partnership goals, for enacting meaningful change strategies, and determining "what will work for us." Even at this early stage of community school development, it is best not to forget that wolves are not really meant to be alone. They live and travel in packs, take care of their young, and protect one another. That's the place where you are trying to get.

Eileen Santiago, former Principal at Thomas Edison Elementary, Port Chester, NY

One of our school's core values is collective responsibility. We have done a lot of work to build cohesion and alignment and to engrain the mindset that community is about collective responsibility. It then becomes much easier to delegate and move away from the idea that there is only one leader and only one person responsible. My leadership team is made up of 14 people. We joke about the fact that everyone is a leader, from the community school coordinator, to the school safety officer, to the school secretary. The same is true with our instructional leadership team (made up of teacher leaders) and our culture and climate team leaders. If these leaders are standing before their team and saying something, that's it. They know I will support them. As principal, I coordinate and make sure everyone is in alignment with our vision, but otherwise, they are the ones in charge. What we do at the school is not rooted in my own belief—this is our school's work—and as a leader, it's one of the most freeing feelings.

Meghan McGoldrick, Principal at the Lilla G. Frederick Pilot Middle School, Boston, MA

Once a vision is defined, clearly articulated, and has received buy-in from the school and community stakeholders, you can immediately use it as the north star for guiding further decisions regarding the school. Those decisions often start with identifying the systems, structures, and processes that can move the school forward; let's look more closely at those in the next chapter.

Notes

1   Many of the ideas in this section came from the following online article: Méndez-Morse (1993). Vision, leadership, and change. Retrieved from https://sedl.org/change/issues/issues23.html. It is a short but

comprehensive compendium of much of the academic literature out there on visionary leadership.
2. Cady, S. H., Wheeler, J. V., DeWolf, J., & Brodke, M. (2011). Mission, vision, and values: What do they say? *Organization Development Journal, 29*(1), 63.
3. Nanus, B. (1992). *Visionary leadership: Creating a compelling sense of direction for your organization*. San Francisco: Jossey-Bass, p. 124.
4. Méndez-Morse (1993). *Vision, leadership, and change*. Retrieved from https://sedl.org/change/issues/issues23.html, but the original research was developed by Nanus, B. (1992). *Visionary leadership: Creating a compelling sense of direction for your organization*. San Francisco: Jossey-Bass, p. 124. It is a short but comprehensive compendium of much of the academic literature out there on visionary leadership. See also Rogus, J. F. (1990). Developing a vision statement—Some considerations for principals. *NASSP Bulletin, 74*(523), 6–12, p. 9; Blokker, J. W. (1989). *Vision, visibility, symbols*. Everett, WA: Professional Development Institute.
5. Nanus, B. (1992). *Visionary leadership: Creating a compelling sense of direction for your organization*. San Francisco: Jossey-Bass, p. 51; Rogus, J. F. (1990). Developing a vision statement—Some considerations for principals. *NASSP Bulletin, 74*(523), 6–12.
6. Nanus, B. (1992). *Visionary leadership: Creating a compelling sense of direction for your organization*. San Francisco: Jossey-Bass, p. 51.
7. Rogus, J. F. (1990). Developing a vision statement—Some considerations for principals. *NASSP Bulletin, 74*(523), 6–12, p. 9.
8. Rogus, J. F. (1990). Developing a vision statement—Some considerations for principals. *NASSP Bulletin, 74*(523), 6–12.
9. Rogus, J. F. (1990). Developing a vision statement—Some considerations for principals. *NASSP Bulletin, 74*(523), 6–12.
10. Spillane, J. P. (2004). *Distributed leadership: What's all the hoopla*. Institute for Policy Research, Northwestern University. Retrieved from http://hub.mspnet.org/index.cfm/9902]
11. Sebring, P. B., & Bryk, A. S. (2000). School leadership and the bottom line in Chicago. *Phi Delta Kappan, 81*(6), 440–443, p. 6.
12. Wheatley, M., & Frieze, D. (2011). Leadership in the age of complexity: From hero to host. *Resurgence Magazine, 264*(January/February), 14–17. Retrieved from https://www.margaretwheatley.com/articles/Leadership-in-Age-of-Complexity.pdf. A big thank you to Ken

Simon, Linda Wheatley, and the IEL team for sharing this work with me at the 2024 National Community Schools and Family Engagement Conference.

13 Wheatley, M., & Frieze, D. (2011). Leadership in the age of complexity: From hero to host. *Resurgence Magazine, 264*(January/February), 14–17. Retrieved from https://www.margaretwheatley.com/articles/Leadership-in-Age-of-Complexity.pdf

14 Wheatley, M., & Frieze, D. (2011). Leadership in the age of complexity: From hero to host. *Resurgence Magazine, 264*(January/February), 14–17. Retrieved from https://www.margaretwheatley.com/articles/Leadership-in-Age-of-Complexity.pdf

15 Wheatley, M., & Frieze, D. (2011). Leadership in the age of complexity: From hero to host. *Resurgence Magazine, 264*(January/February), 14–17. Retrieved from https://www.margaretwheatley.com/articles/Leadership-in-Age-of-Complexity.pdf

16 Wheatley, M., & Frieze, D. (2011). Leadership in the age of complexity: From hero to host. *Resurgence Magazine, 264*(January/February), 14–17. Retrieved from https://www.margaretwheatley.com/articles/Leadership-in-Age-of-Complexity.pdf

17 Wheatley, M., & Frieze, D. (2011). Leadership in the age of complexity: From hero to host. *Resurgence Magazine, 264*(January/February), 14–17. Retrieved from https://www.margaretwheatley.com/articles/Leadership-in-Age-of-Complexity.pdf

18 See https://online.hbs.edu/blog/post/power-mapping-what-it-is-and-how-to-use-it and https://youthnexblog.education.virginia.edu/wp-content/uploads/2023/06/CFCL-Power-Mapping-Activity.pdf

4

Realizing the Vision by Developing and Enhancing Systems and Structures

Introduction

This chapter discusses community school systems and structures. Depending on where you are in your community school journey, you might be developing these structures from the ground up. Alternatively, you may be hoping to build on the systems and structures that are already in place. Regardless of where you are, let's start with three elements that are critical levers in working toward and realizing the school vision: the community school coordinator (CSC or "coordinator"), the needs and assets assessment (NAA) process, and the establishment of a collaborative of integrated partnerships. The chapter will then conclude with a discussion of family engagement versus family involvement.

Community School Coordinator

As a refresher, the community school coordinator (also known in different places as the community school director or community school manager), is a full-time, high-level resource assigned to a single school community whose primary charge is to identify needs and strengths of the community for the purpose of helping students be primed for learning each day in school.

The following quotations underscore why many in the community schools world see the community school coordinator as one of the most important levers in this work.

> My community school coordinator is a role model for the other staff members. He makes things happen. He shows the rest of the school that when they see something that needs to get done, if they really rally the community and put their mind to it, they can find a way to make it happen too. My coordinator also manages all our partnerships. When we have opportunities for new partnerships, they are automatically directed towards him. He does the engagement. He also assesses all of the funding for partnerships and digs deep into whether it makes sense to use our funds in this way. Taking all of this off my plate has been amazing.
>
> **Donette Wilson-Wood**, *Principal at the Haynes Early Learning Center, Boston, MA*

> Thank goodness for my community school coordinator. She runs things by me, I give my input, and then I know I can trust her to do the rest. Recently we were talking about boosting our enrollment. My coordinator brought together a network of school and community leaders who were all putting their heads together about it, and she also created a team to help with a social media campaign. While this work stemmed from our original brainstorming sessions, she takes responsibility and manages the projects from there.
>
> **Casey Campbell**, *Principal at the Cockrill Elementary School, Nashville, TN*

First, we will review what the job of the community school coordinator entails and then discuss some of the characteristics of a great coordinator. Then we'll talk about the role of the principal in building the capacity of the community school coordinator and the importance of investing in the relationship between the principal and CSC.

If the coordinator is a high-level resource, and NOT a pinch-hitting, extra set of hands to cover recess duty—what exactly does that mean? The fact that many districts around the country refer to this person as a community school *director*, versus a community school *coordinator*, is part of the answer. The coordinator is a key partner to the principal, ideally on the same leadership level as the assistant principal or any other top administrator. It is important to note that I believe that *community school director* is the most apt term. However, I will use community school coordinator (or just "coordinator") and the acronym CSC throughout the book, as that was the term that was most widely used by the principals I interviewed.

The reason the coordinator must be a high-level position is that this person is responsible for overseeing many (if not all) of the strategic elements of a community school, including being a sounding-board for the leadership team and serving as the liaison for the entire school staff and outside community. The coordinator is an ambassador who understands "the pulse" of the school and its community. It is a very broad and intense scope of work. In fact, the coordinator often weaves together many of the necessary pieces that principals do not have the bandwidth to execute on their own. There really must be a full-time, high-level staff member to do this work, ideally one whose position is funded for the long term.

The Community Schools Learning Exchange (CSLX)[1] has some great descriptors of what it means to be a community school coordinator—including being a high-level resource (the Chief of Staff!) and an integrator and communicator. In other words, the coordinator is truly the glue (see Table 4.1).

TABLE 4.1 A Community School Coordinator Is…

♦ Like a Chief of Staff; someone who works behind the scenes to solve problems, mediate disputes, and deal with issues before they are brought to the school principal, the "Chief Executive";
♦ An honest broker and truth teller when the school leader needs a wide-ranging view without turf considerations;
♦ An integrator who connects work streams that would otherwise remain siloed;
♦ A communicator who links the leadership team and the broader organization.

There are several key responsibilities that principals noted as inherent in this coordination:

Establishing and convening a Community School Leadership Team: This team or structure is designed to bring various important voices together—both from within the school and beyond school walls. Associated responsibilities include identifying who should be on this team; ensuring diverse representation from parents, students, and community members; and cultivating different skillsets and perspectives. It is this team that supports the needs and assets assessment process.

Spearheading of the needs and assets assessment process through the Community School Leadership team: The coordinator leads the needs and assets assessment process, doing the majority of the legwork, and mobilizing the community school leadership team to engage in all aspects of the process.

Stephanie Ambrose, Principal of the PW Moore elementary school in Elizabeth City, NC, describes how the coordinator runs point, freeing up the principal for other work.

> We conduct a thorough needs assessment process, and then we analyze the results and share them with the community. Those are three discrete and important steps that must happen in community schools. But do principals have the time to do that all by themselves? That's where the community school coordinator comes in. They help craft an assessment that is going to feel relevant, and they

motivate people to buy in and participate in it. It is vital to have a community school coordinator, and it's close to impossible to do this work without one.

In addition to overseeing the multiple steps that Principal Ambrose mentioned, coordinators are also responsible for outreach to and communications with the community about how the assessments inform the school vision. When those who have participated in a needs and assets assessment process see that their input is authentically impacting school behavior, they are more likely to keep contributing. Coordinators are key to building this trust.

Coordinators also serve as what one principal referred to as "key funding go-getters." In other words, the coordinator might use the results of the needs and assets assessment process, namely their community's specific needs and priorities, to seek out potential funding sources in pursuit of achieving the initiative's goals.

Aligning community school strategies with the instructional program: While serving as manager of the community school leadership team, the coordinator should also have a seat on other school teams, including the administrative team and the instructional leadership team (we will talk about these structures in more depth later in the chapter). In that way, they can share information and be the bridge, aligning school priorities and the results of the needs and assets assessment process with the specific responsibilities of community organizations, families, and partners.

As a community school coordinator in the southwest explained,

> Coordinators are the bridge between the academic and non-academic supports on a campus. They are the linchpin. They should feel they have the trust of their school administration to represent their school on campus and throughout their community. The principal's role is to see the coordinator as the conduit— and make sure that there is sacred time allotted to make that happen.

As this coordinator went on to describe, the principal ensures that she has high visibility and access to key leaders. In fact, the principal creates a role for the CSC on their leadership team, has given her the role of Secretary of the Instructional Council, and has her serve on the school attendance team. Being on the Instructional Council, the coordinator helps co-create the agenda to talk about what's going well and the challenges around how community school strategies are being used to accelerate instructional priorities.

Being a recognized presence in the broader community. Several principals, both rural and urban, noted how important it was for their coordinator to get out and be a known presence in the community surrounding their schools. One principal mentioned her coordinator as "doing his own anthropological study" of the school community, trying to understand what is most important to the community and working to identify the most trusted resources for students. The coordinator at a high school in the midwest also talked about the importance of building relationships with families and community members.

> It's not about the money the coordinator brings in—it's about the community schools movement and knowing community members themselves are the experts about their community. The CSC's role is to look at each grant and partner and then listen to the community. This is an all-inclusive decision-making process.

In addition to relationship building, the coordinator ensures that information reaches all staff members within the school so that the entire faculty and staff understands and can be responsive to student needs.

Key Characteristics

Before we go any further, it is important to recognize that coordinators come into their roles with a range of experiences and various levels of familiarity with the community surrounding the school. And as we will discuss shortly, principals must be ready to work through different stages of the relationship with their coordinator.

So what are the key characteristics of a great community school coordinator? What are you looking for during the hiring process? And how do you maintain and nurture that relationship?

First and foremost, there is no single background that community school coordinators need to be successful. Coordinators hail from many walks of life, including schools of social work, the parent community, medical backgrounds, and of course, some are current or former educators.

Shane Dehn (principal at Marion Junior Senior High School in Marion, NY) and Casey Steiner (former principal at Marion Elementary School in Marion, NY and current Director of Community Schools & MTSS for Marion Central School District) shared their thoughts in a conversation together. Principal Dehn stressed the idea of being a self-starter:

> What first comes to mind is that the coordinator must be self-motivated, self-driven, and have that "hungry" mindset, that desire to go find the needs. As principal, we're wearing a lot of different hats and juggling so much at the same time. And we don't always have the time or capacity to say, "here's the need and what we need you to do." If someone has that intrinsic motivation to go find the community need or the school need and dig that out, that for me would be the greatest attribute.

Principal Steiner agreed and also underscored the notion of being a good listener, an idea key to the role that the coordinator must play outside the school walls.

> I agree 100% with the idea of being a self-starter. But I need to share that one of the characteristics of my community school coordinator that makes her so successful is that she listens really well and pays attention to what's happening in the environment—inside and outside the school. She's always observing, always paying attention. As a result, she knows where the needs are and then takes the initiative to make things happen.

Having strong interpersonal skills and both the desire and ability to become enmeshed in the school community are certainly important to this role.

There were several other skills mentioned by principals that must be present or developed in a community school coordinator. I'm going to break them down according to the three-skill approach to leadership shared in Chapter 1.

Conceptual skills (setting a vision and providing strategic direction):

- Understanding of existing school systems and thinking expansively about possible new systems
- Creativity in problem solving
- Synthesizing and integrating action plans

Technical skills (specific knowledge in a given area):

- Analyzing data
- Project management
- Written and oral communication
- Grant-writing

Human skills (relating to and communicating with other people):

- Confidentiality
- Compassion and patience
- Growth mindset
- Persistence and adaptability
- Commitment to developing relationships
- Ability to be a team player

These characteristics and skills can be developed and monitored during meetings with the principal and coordinator (as will be discussed in the next section), and they can also be highlighted through questions asked as part of the hiring process.

A clear theme that principals mentioned was approaching the relationship with their coordinator as a long-term investment—

i.e. taking the time necessary to build the capacity and confidence of the coordinator.

The Relationship between the Principal and Coordinator

Keeping the characteristics of a successful coordinator in mind, let's quickly revisit what many principals noted as key—that the coordinator needs to be a high-level resource, serving as a trusted advisor who provides essential support. As one principal reinforced,

> The community school coordinator is comparable to and should be viewed in the same light as the assistant principal. The org chart must reflect that. The expectation is that the coordinator will support the principal in doing the work that is needed to power the school—it just cannot be that they are an event planner or a recess monitor, which unfortunately, has been the historical experience for some.

Principals also mentioned the critical importance of several elements: a synergy in terms of vision and style and the idea of accessibility and regular communication.

The coordinator and the principal need to be on the same page in terms of the school's vision and the general community school approach. Are they in sync in terms of the systems and structures that need to be developed? Do they have a shared understanding of what it means to be a community school and what is required to make it successful? Do they both understand that community schools are a way of doing business (and are all about systems thinking!) and that community schools are a strategy and not a program?

In addition, there needs to be a synergy of style. As Chris Battaglia, former principal of the Benjamin Franklin High School in Baltimore, MD, and former Director of Community Engagement for Baltimore City Public Schools, offered,

> A principal needs to start by assessing the type of principal that they are. My personality makeup is different from a

lot of my colleagues, and that's not better or worse. But if you have a detail-oriented principal who likes to have the control, you need a coordinator that understands and can work with that mindset. The two personalities need to be able to mesh and work well together.

In addition, the principal must be accessible, and the principal and the coordinator must be in regular communication. An urban principal stressed this idea, along with the notion of eliminating the "principal on high" hierarchy.

You need to have those regular times to meet with your coordinator, and you need to be accessible. I try to be someone who says, "Call me, text me, or we can go for a walk." It's important to move away from a hierarchy, the way that schools are traditionally set up, and instead have a mindset of "I'm here when you need me."

In many schools, the principal meets with the coordinator every week, if not more often. While some interactions may be random—the majority must be regularly scheduled—recognizing that unavoidable conflicts will come up from time to time.

Principal Veronica Sanchez Gregory (Lost Hills Elementary, Lost Hills, CA) understands the importance of both being available and keeping weekly meetings sacred, but she takes it one step further. At the start of every week, Principal Sanchez Gregory asks her coordinator to email her a list of "to-do's" for the week, a list that includes any support she may need from school leadership.

Other principals stress that regular meetings with the coordinator must transcend conversations about how the work is progressing or obstacles they are facing. In fact, the principal and the coordinator must designate time to discuss how the relationship is going and what adjustments are needed.

As Kathleen Provinzano, Associate Professor at Binghamton University, summed up,

> If the relationship between the principal and [the] coordinator is flawed, if the principal thinks everything is fine, and the community school coordinator is totally frustrated because they could never get on the calendar with the principal, then the relationship isn't working in a way that could really be beneficial to the school community.

Accessibility is one important factor, but it is also clear that the relationship between the principal and the coordinator needs to be one that functions at the highest level. Honest and transparent communication is key and should be prioritized by both parties.

Apart from carving out time to communicate, reflect, analyze, and strategize, there are other ways that principals can support their coordinators. Principals can send coordinators to coordinator bootcamps and network gatherings offered by organizations such as the National Center for Community Schools and the Institute for Educational Leadership. Some principals mentioned that they attended the bootcamps *with* their coordinators so that they could process their learnings together and be ready to hit the ground running once they returned to school.

Should your area have a regional training center, you may want to have your coordinator find out what opportunities are available. Often, these training centers can help connect coordinators with others in similar school settings to share insights and problem solve.

A final resource all principals should be aware of is the National Center for Community Schools guide entitled *Leading with Purpose and Passion: A Guide for Community School Directors*.[2] This free resource can serve as an encyclopedia for coordinators, providing practical advice on almost every aspect of their work.

For Schools That Don't Yet Have Funding for a Coordinator

As discussed in Chapter 2, it is important to acknowledge that some schools do not have the resources to immediately support a community school coordinator. An existing staff person, or a small group of staff members, can, on a temporary basis, take on some of the community school responsibilities. This person (or group) can receive training, perhaps from a local regional network, that would enable them to gather some needs and assets assessment data or look at the data already available, and then prioritize and assemble a team to develop an action plan.

But the goal should be that every school has a specifically designated community school coordinator who can maintain firm boundaries around their job responsibilities and be responsible for executing the community school strategies.

Granted, hiring a person whose sole position is that of a community school coordinator does add another line item to the school system's budget. However, there are numerous avenues principals can take to find and maintain funding. We'll discuss those in detail in Chapter 6.

Now that we have a full understanding of what a CSC is and why they are so integral to a community school, let's look at one of the primary concerns of the CSC: the needs and assets assessment process.

The Needs and Assets Assessment Process

The needs and assets assessment process is seen as central to what makes a community school a true community school. Given the importance of this process by which community needs and priorities are determined, let's first revisit our definition from Chapter 2 to ensure we are speaking a common language.

> The needs and assets assessment (NAA) generates information specific to the school and its community that is then used to guide priority setting and the ensuing action plan. Throughout the NAA process, all members of the community, including students, families, and community members, come together to determine community needs, and service gaps, and identify resources that are available to leverage in order to improve student achievement. This process is usually led by the community school coordinator (CSC), in concert with the principal.

What a needs and assets assessment is NOT, is a prescriptive plan that provides random acts of partnerships. Recall the Christmas Tree model mentioned in Chapter 2, where the focus is on collecting lots of new shiny ornaments (programs) that are neither intentional nor organized in any specific way. The needs and assets assessment is designed to create the opposite effect. It determines what students truly need or what communities prioritize and then allows for local input, customization, and ownership.[3]

Michael Essien, former Principal of Martin Luther King Jr. Academic Middle School, San Francisco, CA and current Director of Community Schools and Partnerships for Alameda County Office of Education talked about the components of a needs and assets assessment process and what differentiates a community school from a school with many, but not necessarily integrated, partnerships.

> Many great schools have partnerships. But how you arrive at the partnerships is what determines whether you are a community school or not. You can have thousands of partnerships—but that alone doesn't make you a community school. What makes you a community school is the needs and assets assessment. This assessment is a series of questions given to students, caregivers, families, educators, and organizations that you feel that are part of your community with the goal of uncovering the needs of the various entities. The decision-making body, including students, caregivers, educators, administrators, and people from local organizations, takes the information from this process and then makes decisions and designs intentional partnerships based upon actual needs and priorities. That is a community school.

With this difference firmly in mind, it is equally important to stay focused on the ultimate goal: that of improved student achievement. The analysis of data (both pre-existing and new) by a team of leaders (spearheaded by the community school coordinator) is designed to understand what is enabling student achievement, what is getting in the way, and what stakeholders want most for their school and their students.[4] This information then drives decisions and recommendations about how the community school programming will function. As many principals have shared thus far, the needs and assets assessment process is not something that a principal can take on themselves—it is just too much in addition to all of the principal's other responsibilities. However, the principal can make sure the CSC (or the person assuming that role) has an understanding of the following steps of the process:

1. Pregame: identifying and convening a community school leadership team (if not in place already)
2. Finding existing school and community data
3. Analyzing existing data
4. Collecting new data: surveys, interviews, focus groups
5. Analyzing new data
6. Final data analysis/synthesis
7. Creating a report of findings and recommendations[5]

While we will not go through every step of the process here, let's touch on some of the key elements that principals highlighted as nonnegotiable.

Pre-Game: Getting the Community School Leadership Team in Place

One of the most important first steps is to ensure that the coordinator is ready (and equipped) to assemble a **Community School Leadership Team**. As described in Table 4.2, it is this team, which includes members of the school leadership team, that the CSC will lead through the needs and assets assessment process. There may also be a broader team of partners that meets periodically (sometimes called a **Collaborative Partners Team**); we will talk more about this group of partners in the section about integrated partnerships.

It may be helpful for the principal to sit down with the coordinator and decide which community resources and members might be worth pursuing. Principals mentioned that their leadership teams included people from organizations such as their local recreation department, their community library, the local

TABLE 4.2 Common Team Structures at a Community School[6]

School Leadership Team: This is an internal group of teachers and school leaders that "helps develop school policies and manages the resources needed to implement those policies" and typically oversees the school's Comprehensive Education plan. The community school coordinator holds a decision-making role within this group.

Student Support Teams: There may also be subgroups in which the needs of individual students are discussed and addressed (e.g. MTSS, Pupil Personnel Committee, Student Support Committee).*

Community School Leadership Team: This group is charged with developing and working toward the school vision, implementing the action plan that arises from the needs and assets assessment, and providing oversight. This structure is the foundation of the community school and includes the principal, the School Leadership Team, and other key partners and community members.

Collaborative Partners Team: This team focuses on operationalizing and coordinating partnerships and distributing responsibilities among the partners that comprise the group.

* This is not an exhaustive list; there may be many other teams at any given school.

church, and even a heavily frequented neighborhood store. Getting creative is important.

The UCLA Center for Mental Health in Schools & Student/Learning Supports offers this comprehensive graphic[7] (see Table 4.3) to help coordinators think about the different community assets and resources who could serve as valuable members of a Community School Leadership Team or a Collaborative Partners Team.

With a team in place, you can then focus on finding data for analysis.

Collecting Data

Pre-existing or archival data can provide important information about the population you serve at your school. Before you can make that data useful, you must figure out what is readily available to you. You likely have access to school-level or district-level data on indicators such as chronic absenteeism, attendance rates, discipline/suspension rates, academic performance, graduation rates, and satisfaction/school climate. There may also be city/county data on health, housing, poverty, and crime (to name a few).

TABLE 4.3 A Range of Community Resources That Could Be Part of a Collaborative of Partners

County Agencies and Bodies
(e.g. Departments of Health, Mental Health, Children and Family Services, Public Social Services, Probation, Sheriff, Office of Education, Fire, Service Planning Area Councils, Recreation & Parks, Library, courts, housing)

Municipal Agencies and Bodies
(e.g. parks and recreation, library, police, fire, courts, civic event units)

Physical and Mental Health and Psychological Concerns, Facilities, and Groups
(e.g. hospitals, clinics, guidance centers, Aid to Victims, MADD, "Friends of" groups; family crisis and support centers, helplines, hotlines, shelters, mediation and dispute resolution centers)

Mutual Support/Self-Help Groups
(e.g. for almost every problem and many other activities)

Child Care/Preschool Centers

Postsecondary Education Institution/ Students
(e.g. community colleges, state universities, public and private colleges and universities, vocational colleges, specific schools within these such as Schools of Law, Education, Nursing, Dentistry)

Sports/Health/Fitness/Outdoor Groups
(e.g. sports teams, athletic leagues, local gyms, conservation associations, Audubon Society)

Community-Based Organizations
(e.g. neighborhood and homeowners' associations, Neighborhood Watch, block clubs, housing project associations, economic development groups, civic associations)

Faith Community Institutions
(e.g. congregations and subgroups, clergy associations, Interfaith Hunger Coalition)

Legal Assistance groups
(e.g. Public Counsel, schools of law)

Ethnic Associations
(e.g. Committee for Armenian Students in Public Schools, Korean Youth Center, United Cambodian Community, African-American, Latino, Asian-Pacific, Native American Organizations)

Special Interest Associations and Clubs
(e.g. Future Scientists and Engineers of America, pet owner and other animal-oriented groups)

(*Continued*)

TABLE 4.3 A Range of Community Resources That Could Be Part of a Collaborative of Partners (*Continued*)

Service Agencies (e.g. PTA/PTSA, United Way, clothing and food pantries, Visiting Nurses Association, Cancer Society, Catholic Charities, Red Cross, Salvation Army, volunteer agencies, legal aid society)	*Arts and Cultural Institutions* (e.g. museums, art galleries, zoo, theater groups, motion picture studios, TV and radio stations, writers' organizations, instrumental/choral)
Service Clubs and Philanthropic Organizations (e.g. Lions Club, Rotary Club, Optimists, Assistance League, men's and women's clubs, veteran's groups, foundations)	*Businesses/Corporations/Unions* (e.g. neighborhood business associations, chambers of commerce, local shops, restaurants, banks, AAA, Teamsters, school employee unions)
Youth Agencies and Groups (e.g. Boys and Girls Clubs, Y's, Scouts, 4-H, Woodcraft Rangers)	*Media* (e.g. newspapers, TV and radio, local access cable)
	Family members, local residents, senior citizen groups

In the next section, we'll focus mainly on the collection of new data, not the archival or pre-existing data, as this new information (collected from the community being served by the school) will be the key driver of practice. Principals shared some of their best approaches for finding that data.

Mark Gaither, Principal of Wolfe Street Academy in Baltimore, MD, explained that before even starting to ask questions for the needs and assets assessment, it was important to make sure that community members understood (or were reacquainted with) what community schools are and why their voice in the process matters.

> If this is the school's first needs and assets assessment process, the first step is to explain what a community school is. This can be done in-person, virtually, pre-recorded virtually, or there can even be links to what a community school is in action or on the internet that parents and other stakeholders can go see. Anything from good old flyers home in the backpack is a great means of getting the word

out. There really isn't anything that should be held back. The folks new to the idea need to see the breadth and possibilities of what it could be. In pre-existing community schools, it's about getting more community members involved and even sometimes re-explaining what community schools are.

To ensure that the community understands what community schools are and why being a part of this data collection process is so pivotal, some principals mentioned adding an aspirational component to their questioning. Where does the staff and community want to be in five years? What are their hopes, dreams, desires, and wants? Knowing that the hard questions about barriers need to be asked, how can you push this work beyond just filling gaps, and rather about creating opportunities?

Additionally, Chris Coan, Principal at Parker Elementary in Panama City, FL, spoke about the importance of making sure that this collecting step of the NAA process was not just about mining for surface level data. He explained,

> There are schools that are only looking at that icing level of the cake. They're not really getting in and realizing, there's more in this that's way deeper. I'm starting to see that now as we've finally removed the top layer of cake. It's like, "Oh, I didn't realize this was inside." Well, in people, you may know the top two layers. But then there's that next layer that you had no idea existed. And that may truly be the root or core of the problem. And it's like, oh, I got it now. We can definitely say with some of our families that we have found that core, and we've had incredible success stories.

Principal Gaither offered specific questions and prompts, some of which could be asked on surveys or in focus groups designed to gather qualitative data. These questions are framed in the context of "What does our community school need to do to serve our students and families?"

1. What is the strongest or best part of your child? Family? Neighborhood? School? City?
2. What are our greatest academic, social, and neighborhood challenges?
3. Share a positive experience you have had in the past year with another member of your community.
4. Share a negative experience you have had in the past year with another member of your community.
5. What do you see as the biggest barrier to your child's/student's success?

In terms of getting more voices involved, other principals offered strategies such as carving out time in school for students to complete their component of the assessment and giving all classes with 100% survey completion rates a pizza party. Another principal found that a combination of paper and online surveys yielded the highest completion rates for families. And yet another principal mentioned that a hugely effective practice in his school was giving the student government some ownership in the data collection process. As he aptly noted, it is difficult to say no to persistent students.

Once the needs are identified and codified, it's time to look at the assets currently available to the school that might fulfill those needs.

Matching Needs to Resources

In the first few chapters of this book, we emphasized that community schools are an asset-based model—not a deficit-based model. So, it makes sense that a good place to start matching needs to resources is with a brainstorming session with your coordinator about the different types of assets that your community (whether rural or urban) might have available to work with.

As Jerry Johnson, Phoebe Moore Dail Distinguished Professor in Rural Education at East Carolina University, explained,

In urban places, assets might be brick and mortar facilities. In rural places, they're more likely to be nature-related or people-focused. What I find when I do asset mapping in rural settings is that human assets are at a premium in a way that they're not in urban places. You may not have a Children's Museum, but you do have someone who was a major figure in the Civil Rights movement, or you have a retired forest ranger who can come in and teach wonderful lessons on wildlife preservation. So, when you think about what kinds of assets are there, as a principal, you need to recognize that the process is the same, but it's going to look very different in an urban setting than it is in a rural setting.

The conversation where the principal, coordinator, and the Community School Leadership Team mobilize assets and resources to meet documented needs is a critically important lever in the needs and assets assessment process. It is also a central tenet of the community schools strategy. To help facilitate that conversation, the Community School Leadership team may want to engage in asset mapping—a process for identifying the strengths and resources of the surrounding community. The resources that emerge from this process can then help inform programmatic decisions. If a need or priority emerges from the needs and assets assessment, it can then be matched to a community resource. In addition, this process (especially if it involves multiple stakeholders) can help mobilize, motivate, and empower community members to get more involved in helping realize the school's vision.

Throughout this and all phases of the NAA, principals should be ready to offer guidance and coaching. However, everyone must always remember that it requires a collective effort.

A Team Effort

Thinking about the NAA process as a whole can feel overwhelming. However, pooling resources to support a school is at the very heart of community schools. Coordinators can keep the overwhelm at a minimum by remembering they are part of an ever-expanding team. At some schools, the coordinator reaches out to partners such as a local university to help with the data collection. Others may already be paired with a university in some capacity that may be able to help analyze the needs and assets assessment data (some may even already be considered a university-assisted community school!).

Former Principal Ann Hanna (Community School Consultant in the Maine Department of Education and Former Principal at Gerald E. Talbot Community School, Portland, ME) explained how she was able to engage a university to help with the workload.

> The biggest message is that you need people on your team that can help lift the work. During our planning years, we partnered with the University of Southern Maine, who gave us access to a group of graduate fellows in their data innovation project. These fellows played a key role in helping our team organize and make sense of the data from our needs and assets assessment. We were doing surveys in multiple different languages and the information from both the surveys and the in-person focus groups was just so much—we didn't quite know what to do with it. The university's ability to analyze the data and present it to us in a clear and comprehensible manner made all the difference.

Another principal shared that she brought in a local nonprofit to help with the data analysis. She also mentioned how beneficial it was to tap into some of the national community school resources, including those provided by the National Education Association (NEA).

Although the coordinator is at the center of the needs and assets assessment process, the practice should be engrained within the entire school. As Jo Gomes, Senior Director of Boston Community Hub Schools, YMCA of Greater Boston, explained,

> The needs and assets assessment is not just for the community school coordinator or the administrative team. It's a way to transform a school. Every member of the school should know that their school is a community school and understand their role within it. School leaders aren't

being asked to carry "yet another thing" but really transform the way a school community thinks and functions.

The National Center for Community Schools has compiled a comprehensive tool kit,[8] shared in Appendix C. It offers key strategies and steps for each step of the NAA process that a principal can download, share, and discuss with their coordinator. This resource has been adapted by many states and cities to meet their local contexts and is truly a lifesaver. But beware: doing an NAA is not a one-and-done process; it will need to be repeated at future intervals to ensure relevance.

How frequently should the NAA be administered?

Principals mentioned that trying to do a comprehensive needs and assets assessment every year might be too labor-intensive. Several recommended a cycle in which an in-depth NAA is conducted every two or three years or whenever there has been a change in circumstances (e.g. a new lead agency, a new community school coordinator, or a new principal).

They also suggested that in the "off years," the coordinator conducts periodic check-ins with different representatives from constituent groups, keeping their "finger on the pulse in a day-to-day kind of way" as one principal referred to it. The relationships that a great CSC or principal has built within the community can yield information about community strengths and needs, regardless of whether there was a comprehensive NAA process that year.

From a Co-Located Partner to an Integrated, Collaborative System

Now that we've moved through the needs and assets assessment process, what happens next? How do you determine which partners are the right ones? What else is true of partners in a community school? And what conditions need to be cultivated?

Let's start by breaking down the two different types of partnerships that can happen at a school. The first is more traditional: the co-located partner. The co-located partner is a service provider who comes into the school and operates in their own separate lane. This provider is typically not connected to the school day or already existing school programming—they are working in parallel with the school and other partners. The second is the community schools version: the integrated partner. With the integrated partner, the partner becomes part of the fabric of school life. This partner meets at regular intervals with school staff to talk about students' challenges and accomplishments and to ensure that their programming is aligned with student needs.

In community schools, partners are far more than tenants in the school building; in fact, integrated partners are standard practice. But in some of the most mature community schools, principals describe their partners as coming together to form a collaborative. Partners, of course, work in conjunction with the school, but here they also work together to create a new system of support for students in which the end results are greater than the sum of their parts. It is when partnerships become a collaborative that the systemic work true to community schools comes into play.

So what is required for a partner to fulfil their responsibilities as a service provider AND be a part of an integrated system or collaborative? To start, it is critical to choose partners based on the needs and priorities that arise through the NAA process. But that alone is not enough. Partners must:

1. Have value systems that reflect those of the school,
2. Show a clear commitment to moving the school closer to its vision,
3. Be willing to be held accountable for this movement.

Many principals noted the necessity of having a clear memorandum of understanding (MOU) with each partner, even though developing MOUs can be a time-consuming process. Here, the added capacity of the community school coordinator is a key.

These MOUs are designed to do several things—first, delineate duties and financial responsibilities specific to the individual partnership and ensure protection from liabilities. Terms may include enrollment processes and limitations, use of space, and types of services provided. This document may transcend the school context and involve signatures and buy in from the Superintendent, School Board, or Mayor.

Ideally, the MOU also will include what it means to be part of the collaborative, or the system as a whole. That requires carving out time for individual partners to align their work with that of other partners and with the school academic leadership team. But perhaps most importantly, the MOU is also designed to ensure that the partnership is "leader-proof," that it continues to exist and thrive even if there are changes in leadership or staffing.

An Integrated System

While the first steps can be partnership selection and the development of a clear memorandum of understanding with each partner, questions remain about how to create a system that effectively aligns partners with each other and the school. What are the systems for ensuring that struggling students are involved in the right partnerships for them? Is a student identified at risk for substance abuse involved in multiple parallel programs, neither in contact with the other?[9] What are the systems for ensuring that students are getting coordinated supports? And, are partners truly committed to moving the school vision forward?

Bringing partners together in order to build new and stronger systems is no easy task. Carving out the time and space to meet (which can often seem at odds with the time spent working directly with students and families) requires creativity and persistence.

Principal Claudia DeLarios Morán shares a simple step that helps with this coordination:

> Our community school coordinator arranges a monthly meeting that's just for our resource providers, all the organizations that connect with our school, to make sure that we're all aligned, meeting the same goals, and not at cross purposes. So whether you're an organization that pushes into the afterschool program to provide literacy support or if you're a soccer club that's working with our students or the chess guy who comes in on Thursdays during lunch, everybody who is

touching our students comes to this meeting. Everyone needs to understand what the vision is and how each entity is linking up to it. During this time, we also share what's working, what's not, and what needs to be adjusted.

The flyer below from a community school in Boston shares sample information for a fall introductory meeting for all school partners (see Figure 4.1)

Migdalia Cortes (Community School Director at Salome Urena Campus Community School for the Children's Aid Society) has a yearly plan for bringing partners together around the school vision that she shares here:

At the end of August, even before teachers come back, we hold collaborative planning meetings for all our

FIGURE 4.1 Partnership Round Table[10]

partners. At this first meeting, we sit down and share our school vision and partnership vision for the year, and we talk about how their services fit into and align with those visions. We then have quarterly meetings for the remainder of the year. Our first quarterly meeting in the fall is to look at data from the past year and set our goals for the year ahead. What are the outcomes we want to reach in areas such as attendance, parent engagement, and social emotional learning? At our next meetings, we talk about progress toward those goals and the role that each partner has played that quarter to move closer to those goals. It really is a marriage, and the foundation needs to be set at the beginning of the year.

As Claudia DeLarios Morán shared earlier and Community School Director Torres just shared with us, partners must understand the school's vision and their role in achieving it. They must also understand how they can work together to support specific students and groups of students. Finally, there must be systems and procedures by which these conversations occur and how problems are solved in place for facilitating those conversations and solving problems. Here are different questions that the collaborative may want to answer together:

- What does it mean to be aligned with this school's vision?
- What does the partner vetting process look like?
- What is my specific role as part of this collaborative?
- What are my responsibilities as part of this collaborative?
- How do I know what other supports students in my program are getting?
- How do I know what students are at particular risk?
- What happens when there is a conflict between the school and one of the partners? What happens when there is conflict between the partners? What are the mechanisms for conflict resolution?
- How do new partners get onboarded to this collaborative? What protocols has the group put in place?[11]

One of the goals of creating a collaborative is to elevate the role of support providers, seeing them, alongside school staff and teachers, as a connected and a critical part of the school ecosystem. One way of doing this is to include partners in schoolwide professional development or even having partners facilitate or lead specific sessions for school staff.[12] Being connected to teaching and learning ensures that service providers are not seen as parallel partners, but rather an integral part of realizing the school vision.

Parent and Community Engagement versus Involvement

This chapter now moves from the engagement of partners to the engagement of families. Carlos Azcoitia, former Principal at John Spry Community School and Community Links High School (a prek-12 model), Chicago, IL, reminds us of how it all fits together.

> We understand that the greatest influence on the student is the family and the greatest influence on the family is the community. So for a school to be successful, you have to connect that trilogy—the family, the community, and the student.

If the greatest influence on the student is the family, it makes sense that powerful student and family engagement is a key tenet of community schools. But what exactly makes engagement powerful? It may be helpful to start with a simple distinction, namely, *what is the difference between parent engagement and parent involvement?* Simply put, parent engagement is more along the lines of "doing with" parents and parent involvement is "doing to."[13] Parent involvement is transactional- parents are contacted and parents are asked to contribute. While parents may volunteer or attend parent teacher conferences, these actions are typically controlled by the school. There may even be some elements of a deficit model that come into play here, as there may be an inclination to "fix broken" parents and guardians. In contrast, parent engagement is when parents are truly engaged with the work of the school. They have a real say and input in how the school makes some of its decisions. Parent engagement assumes an asset-based mindset, as the parents are seen as critical contributors to these conversations. In fact, as Ann Ishimaru, a highly esteemed researcher of transformative parent engagement, explains: their voices are not just appreciated, rather "they provide cultural and intellectual resources that can contribute to transforming instructional and institutional practices in schools."[14]

Another way of thinking about it is in terms of reciprocal, or two-way conversations with families. In these conversations, the school is not the only expert on teaching and nurturing children; rather, the family is also seen as an important resource. As Ellen Lloyd, former principal (Marion Elementary, Marion NY and current superintendent of Marion Schools), explained,

> A real question we grappled with was whether we knew our families and were learning from our families. What does our outreach look like? And even though we were putting out tons of flyers, social media posts, and weekly emails, there was no dialogue—no real conversations with family members.
>
> So we made a really concerted effort around reciprocal communication, which we defined as a meaningful two-way interaction with a parent, either a face to face conversation, a phone conversation, or an email exchange. At the elementary level, we decided that having 100% communication with our families, three times a year, was going to be one of our main goals. Can we guarantee that we've had reciprocal communication with 100% of our families? If we haven't listened to our families, do we really know what the needs are? And we mean all families, not just the ones who are going to respond to our surveys or come to the PTO events.

The next level of parent engagement is when parents actually have some control over decision-making. Examples might be serving on the Community School Leadership Team, playing a leadership role in developing "parent academies," where parents themselves focus on issues that they deem important, or when schools can share goals with parents and then involve them directly in realizing them.

The project-based learning coach at Lavaland Elementary (Albuquerque, NM) shared, on a small scale, an example of creative parent outreach and engagement.

> This past May, we invited parents in to help us plan what a community event would look like in the fall. We wanted them, not us, as educators, to help decide what the community needs. What do *they* want to see? The parents came up with the idea that for each grade level, the kids would create a game. That way, they would be the ones that are driving it and marketing it. The kids were the ones who said, "Hey, come see my game!" and we ended up getting far more parents to attend than we would have otherwise.

The principal can also play a role in getting the staff more aware of external events and community happenings. As one principal mentioned,

> Opportunities to engage families do not have to happen in the school building. They can occur in our community, at community events, and at neighborhood functions. The principal and [the] coordinator need go about creating meaningful family engagement in different ways.

For interactions within the school, there may be a number of logistical barriers that the principal needs to work through. Is the school truly open to family members? Is the sign-in process manageable? Do families feel welcomed by the first people they meet when they come into the school?

It is important to also consider other barriers to communication. How do you, as principal, and in support of the coordinator, effectively get your message out and ensure that parents show up? How can you reinforce the idea that their voice matters?

What does it look like when you keep that message in the forefront? When parents leave school events, do they feel as though they are more a part of the school than previously or did they just attend a nice gathering? It is important for the principal and the coordinator to carve out time to determine what processes and procedures need to shift in order to engage families, and what new systems can be constructed to move from parent involvement to parent engagement.

❓ Responses from Principals in the Field

What systems can you put in place so that the collaborative is truly collaborating?

Once you have determined who your partners are going to be, then you and your coordinator need to bring them together around your vision and a shared plan of action. It is important to remember that partners also need to share ways in which they can advance and support each other's missions. Our team would meet monthly with partners, after school hours and during the summer, and we included two teacher volunteers, who also served on the Community School Advisory Board. At times we were able to set aside money from the superintendent's allocated budget to stipend participants for this work, especially when we focused specifically on tiered interventions for individual students or groups of youngsters with similar needs or when we needed to review instructional initiatives. These discussions would address the commonalities across partners and how they could use each other as resources.

We were also able to negotiate a day of non-attendance for the children, toward the end of the year, where faculty and partners came together. We would always begin the day with fun team-building experiences and then partners and different faculty committees would give a presentation on what had been accomplished that year—what types of services and instructional initiatives were being provided, what outcomes they were observing, and what the various forms of data collection had demonstrated. At one of our retreats, a panel of parents joined our faculty and partners to speak about their own experiences in schools they had attended primarily in other countries and what they wanted for their children in America. All of these presentations were very powerful and served to strengthen our collaborative commitment to our community school.

(Eileen Santiago, former Principal of Thomas Edison Elementary, Port Chester, NY)

—

The principal leads the process of creating the vision for the school, under the board and under the district leadership, and then aligning everyone, including all the partners, around the vision. It must be a cohesive team. In fact, the students at Oyler felt like the partners were part of Cincinnati Public Schools (CPS). They just assumed that Miss Jami worked for CPS and at the dental center, people worked for CPS, and so on and so forth. I wouldn't have a staff meeting or gathering without inviting all of the partners, as they need to be at the table. Partners really were integrated into the school community, which initially could have been time consuming, but it saves you at the end of the day because you're not constantly stopping someone and saying, "Wait a minute, that doesn't align with our school vision." Investing time in bringing partners together with school staff led to conversations that changed the whole game for us. Our seamless collaboration of teachers, partners, families, and all stakeholder groups had a significant impact on students, ranging from academics to medical support to stable housing.

(Amy Randolph, former Principal of Oyler School, Pre k-12, Cincinnati Ohio, and current Assistant Superintendent, Cincinnati Public Schools

Now that we have covered the crucial role of the community school coordinator, the needs and assets assessment process, the power of a collaborative of integrated partners, and the importance of parent engagement, we will now turn our attention to data, evaluation, and funding.

Notes

1. CSLX. (2023). *The basics: Community school coordinator.* Retrieved from https://cslx.org/resources/the-basics-community-school-coordinator
2. NCCS. (2017). *Leading with purpose and passion: A guide for community school directors.* Retrieved from https://www.nccs.org/wp-content/uploads/2021/10/NCCS_CS_Directors_Guide_compressed.pdf
3. This sentence was adapted from the *Community Schools Playbook*. Retrieved from https://communityschools.futureforlearning.org
4. Santiago, E., Ferrara, J., & Quinn, J. (2012). *Whole child, whole school: Applying theory to practice in a community school.* Lanham, MD: Rowman & Littlefield.
5. Adapted from NCCS resource: https://www.nccs.org/publication/asssets-needs-assessment-toolkit/
6. New Mexico Public Education Department. (2024). *The site based leadership team.* Retrieved from https://webnew.ped.state.nm.us/bureaus/community-schools-and-extended-learning/community-schools/key-practices/key-practice-2/the-site-based-leadership-team/#:~:text=The%20Site%20Based%20Leadership%20Team%20is%20the%20foundation%20of%20a,participatory%20practices%20for%20distributing%20responsibilities; CSLX. (2023). *The basics: Community school coordinator.* Retrieved from https://cslx.org/resources/the-basics-community-school-coordinator
7. Adelman, H. S., & Taylor, L. (2021). *Evolving community schools and transforming student/learning supports.* Los Angeles: Center for MH in Schools & Student/Learning Supports at UCLA. Retrieved from https://smhp.psych.ucla.edu/pdfdocs/evolvecomm.pdf
8. National Center for Community Schools. (2024). *Needs assessment tool kit.* Retrieved from https://www.nccs.org/publication/asssets-needs-assessment-toolkit/
9. Adelman, H. S., & Taylor, L. (2021). *Evolving community schools and transforming student/learning supports.* Los Angeles: Center for MH in Schools & Student/Learning Supports at UCLA. Retrieved from https://smhp.psych.ucla.edu/pdfdocs/evolvecomm.pdf
10. This flyer was created by Michaiah Lopez, Community School Coordinator at the Dr. Albert D. Holland High School of Technology, Boston, MA.

11 Adelman, H. S., & Taylor, L. (2021). *Evolving community schools and transforming student/learning supports.* Los Angeles: Center for MH in Schools & Student/Learning Supports at UCLA. Retrieved from https://smhp.psych.ucla.edu/pdfdocs/evolvecomm.pdf

12 Partnership for the Future of Learning. (2018). *Community schools playbook.* Retrieved from https://communityschools.futureforlearning.org

13 Ferlazzo, L. (2012). *Response: The difference between parent "involvement" & parent "engagement.* Retrieved from https://www.edweek.org/leadership/opinion-response-the-difference-between-parent-involvement-parent-engagement/2012/03

14 Ishimaru, A. M. (2019). From family engagement to equitable collaboration. *Educational Policy, 33*(2), 350–385, p. 357.

5

Building a Sound Foundation: Data, Evaluation, and Funding

Introduction

Whether improving instruction, determining readiness to learn, ensuring appropriate student supports, or showing the broader world that what the school is doing is making a difference, my guess is that it would be close to impossible for any principal to avoid data-driven practices. However, there is a big difference between being a data champion and being a more passive participant in the world of data. And when you factor in the work at a community school, involving broader systems and a more diverse group of stakeholders, the conversation becomes increasingly complex. This chapter explores how data is used in the community school context to elevate practice and create a cycle of continuous improvement.

How Are Data and Evaluation Different at a Community School?

We've already covered quite a bit about data in the previous chapters. Chapter 4 explored the collection and synthesis of archival and emerging data, both within and outside the school, to inform the needs and assets assessment process. Chapter 3 examined how collaborative leadership structures enable different groups of faculty and community members to use data to brainstorm and problem solve.

Before we go any deeper, let's first cover two major assumptions that must frame our thinking about data in the community school context. The first, covered in the introduction, is that out-of-school influences, such as a student's socioeconomic background and status, are more important contributors to academic outcomes than just about anything else, even extensive funding. Factors, including limited medical care and food insecurity, may account for as much as two-thirds of the difference in academic outcomes.[1] So, when thinking about data through a community school lens, multiple metrics must be considered on the path to improving academic and other results.

The second assumption is that the responsibility for looking at data and evaluating progress cannot lie solely in the hands of the principal and/or the highest tier of academic leadership. The principal must set up systems and structures by which teams of staff and community partners come together to look at changes in a number of metrics, all of which are driven by the school's vision. Data must be a team sport.

But most importantly, a significant mindset shift must occur in terms of how community school leaders approach data. As Jonathan Cohen, from the National School Climate Center, explained during an interview, "Educators are now accustomed to data being used as a hammer."[2] In other words, data becomes a more punitive measure, a barometer of whether people are "getting the job done." While there is nothing wrong with accountability measures, in a community school, data becomes more of a flashlight. It is used not just to identify problems but to shed light on possible solutions. In a community school, data must be seen as a positive lever for change.

Michael Essien, former Principal of Martin Luther King Jr. Academic Middle School, San Francisco, CA, and current Director of Community Schools and Partnerships for Alameda County Office of Education reinforced the idea that data is not just about determining who has dropped the proverbial ball. He explained how data can fuel the cycle for continuous improvement:

> Data is how you make meaning. It's not how you hold people accountable. It's the conversation for change. It's the conversation for assessing your systems and structures—your mission and vision for areas of strength and opportunities for growth. Once you understand that and get the right individuals at the table, all kinds of conversations can occur in order to change and transform your learning environment at school.

Let's now revisit the first assumption, where academic achievement cannot be seen in isolation.

Figure 5.1[3] puts forward a number of results, both short-term and longer-term, that are at the heart of academic success. Short-term results include school readiness, consistent attendance, the involvement of families and communities in school life, and student engagement in learning.

Longer-term results include the obvious, such as students' academic success as shown in grade-level promotion and graduation rates, and then others, such as mental and physical health, safe and supportive learning environments, and ultimately family and community wellness. This table also includes important indicators for measuring progress toward these results.

An urban principal spoke to the importance of using a diverse range of indicators, such as those illustrated in this table, that ultimately contribute to academic success.

> Typically, impact is measured using hard numbers or quantitative data. With the community schools strategy, you wrap that data in the stories of the families, students, and everyone who is part of that school community. When kids feel safe and like they belong, when teachers feel empowered and are enjoying their time with the kids, when parents are engaged and have a partnership with a school that is meaningful—which are the types of things that the community school strategy lends itself to and

CONDITIONS FOR LEARNING	RESULTS	INDICATORS	
		SHORT TERM	
1. Early childhood development is fostered through high-quality, comprehensive programs that nurture learning and development.	CHILDREN ARE READY TO ENTER SCHOOL	• Immunization rates • Blood lead levels • Parents read to children • Children attend early childhood programs	• Receptive vocabulary level • Families connected to support networks/services • Vision, hearing and dental status
2. The school has a core instructional program with qualified teachers, a challenging curriculum, and high standards and expectations for students.	STUDENTS ATTEND SCHOOL CONSISTENTLY	• Daily attendance • Early chronic absenteeism • Tardiness • Truancy	
3. Students are motivated and engaged in learning–both in school and in community settings, during and after school.	STUDENTS ARE ACTIVELY INVOLVED IN LEARNING AND THE COMMUNITY	• Students feel they belong in school • Availability of in-school and after-school programs • Students feel competent • Schools are open to community	• Attendance at before and after-school programs • Partnerships for service learning in the school/community • Post-secondary plans
4. The basic physical, social, emotional and economic needs of young people and their families are met.	SCHOOLS ARE ENGAGED WITH FAMILIES AND COMMUNITIES	• Trust between faculty and families • Teacher attendance and turnover • Faculty believe they are an effective and competent team • Community-school partnerships	
5. There is mutual respect and effective collaboration among parents, families and school staff.	FAMILIES ARE ACTIVELY INVOLVED IN CHILDREN'S EDUCATION	• Families support students' education at home • Family attendance at school wide events and parent teacher conferences	• Family experience with school wide events and classes • Family participation in school decision making
6. The community is engaged in the school and promotes a school climate that is safe, supportive and respectful and that connects students to a broader learning community.		**LONGTERM**	
	STUDENTS SUCCEED ACADEMICALLY	• Standardized test scores • Teachers support students • Grades • Teachers take positive approach to teaching and learning	• Graduation rates • Dropout rates • Reading by 3rd grade
	STUDENTS ARE HEALTHY PHYSICALLY, SOCIALLY AND EMOTIONALLY	• Asthma control • Vision, hearing and dental status • Physical fitness • Nutritional habits	• Positive adult relationships • Positive peer relationships
	STUDENTS LIVE AND LEARN IN STABLE AND SUPPORTIVE ENVIRONMENTS	• Students staff and families feel safe • Schools are clean • Families provide for basic needs	• Incidents of bullying • Reports of violence or weapons
	COMMUNITIES ARE DESIRABLE PLACES TO LIVE	• Employment and employability of residents and families served by the school • Student and families with health insurance	• Community mobility and stability • Juvenile crime

FIGURE 5.1 Community Schools Framework for Student Success

that need to be accounted for—that's when the school becomes a hub of the community, not just a place where a child is sent to learn.

What is clear is that hard, quantitative academic data cannot alone drive a community school strategy. But how does an individual school drill down into what is important to it? For most schools, a logic model is the tool of choice. Many principals may already be familiar with the concept of a logic model or even have one in place for their school. For those of you who do not, this next section is for you. As an added incentive, it's worth noting that all submissions for the federal government's Full-Service Community School's Grant Awards Program require a logic model to be included in their application.

How to Create a Logic Model[4]

To start, a logic model is a visual tool that provides a quick snapshot of how strategies or resources translate into the achievement of a goal. Another way of describing the logic model is that it captures the relationship between what you are planning to do and the intended effects.

The process of creating a logic model and the logic model itself serve several key data functions: it spotlights exactly what data needs to be collected in order to demonstrate the achievement of desired results, it helps build a shared understanding of what you are trying to achieve and measure for a broad swath of stakeholders, and it helps set up action plans to improve practice.[5]

In its simplest form, the logic model (see Figure 5.2) does this by listing what's needed to drive or support a program or strategy (the Inputs), the actual activities that happen during the process (the Activities), and the intended results (the Outcomes).[6]

Other logic models include an additional category for Outputs (what product or service is delivered or what strategy is used), along with a category for Outcomes. Often, the Outcome

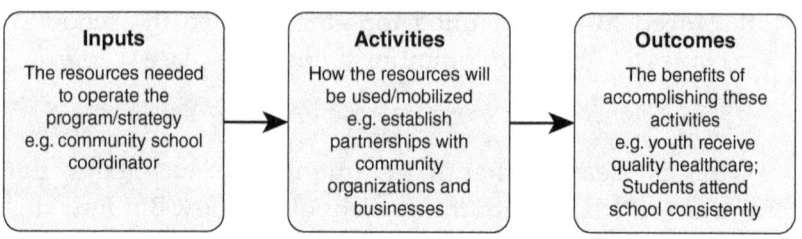

FIGURE 5.2 Inputs, Activities, and Outcomes

category is divided into both short- and long-term outcomes as shown in Figure 5.3.

Simply put, the logic model illustrates the connection among the strategies, the work planned, and the short- and long-term results so that you can monitor progress and setbacks and share the state of play with other stakeholders.

The Logic Model and the School Vision

If the logic model is a way of articulating how your community school system will function, it then makes sense that the entire logic model must stem from the vision we talked about in Chapter 3. If the vision combines a clear direction or a goal with a plan for achieving it, then the vision provides the framework for all of the logic model—determining the desired outcomes and then working backward to determine which activities and strategies will be most effective in reaching your goals.

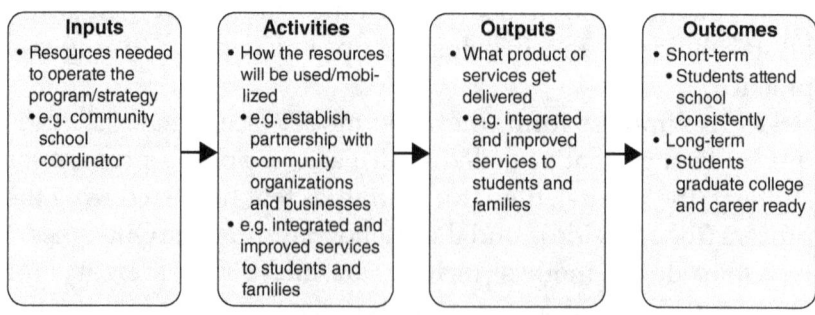

FIGURE 5.3 Inputs, Activities, Outputs, and Outcomes

Principal Claudia DeLarios Morán (Buena Vista Horace Mann K-8, San Francisco, CA) reinforced the importance of starting with the vision, as well as showing how the work set forth in the vision and the logic model must drive and inform communications throughout the year:

> Starting with the vision, you need to ask yourself, what are we charged to do through this vision? What are the goals that we want to achieve and the targets that we want to meet? What are the initiatives that we are going to launch this year, and then what are the goals that show how we are going to measure our effectiveness? It is essential that you share this all in your school site council meetings. You share it in your family newsletters. You share it in your weekly staff bulletins. You share it out in your staff meetings at the beginning of the school year, and you consistently return to those themes over the course of the year. You're constantly broadcasting what your larger initiatives are and your progress towards meeting your goals. If we don't follow this pattern, we get lost in too many competing things that occur daily in school. We lose the thread. Part of the job of the administrator at a community school really is to remind people, all the time, why we're doing what we're doing and where we are trying to go.

Often, the vision or mission is included atop the logic model, as shown in Figure 5.4.

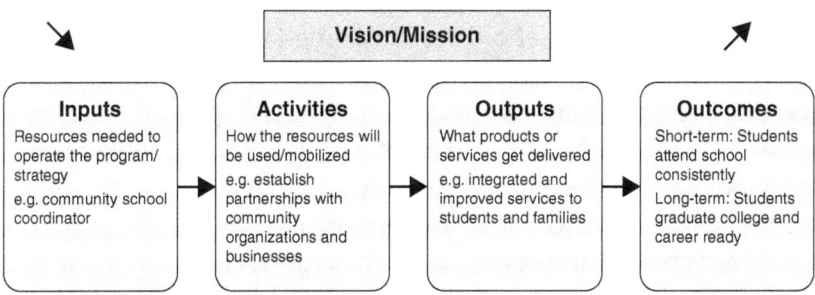

FIGURE 5.4 Logic Model Linked to Vision and Mission

Sample Logic Models

The following logic model (see Figure 5.5) was created by the Institute for Educational Leadership and the Coalition for Community Schools[7]. The traditional *activities* column is replaced with a *what can happen at a community school* column, and it includes separate columns for short- and long-term results. Finally, the impact column at the far right includes a "direction or goal" element of the vision statement.

The second logic model (see Figure 5.6) comes from Fairfax County.[8] Its impact statement, like that of the previous logic model, contains the "direction or goal" element of a vision statement.

The final logic model (see Figure 5.7) provides an example highlighting a rural context. This model includes an impact column, an activities column (referred to as strategies), the traditional output column, and two separate columns for short- and long-term outcomes. What is noticeable here is that the short- and long-term outcomes are very specific and measurable, in contrast to the two previous logic models. It also includes a column at the far right that names overall impacts on the school and community.[9]

These logic models are designed to stimulate your thinking about possible applications to your own school context or how you can build on what you already have in place. Ultimately, the goal is to determine, through this model, whether your school is improving over time according to the carefully selected metrics and whether it is implementing community school strategies effectively.

Similar to the vision, a logic model becomes more than a graphic or a document when it is brought to life and owned by a broad group of stakeholders, including families, students, and the greater community. Creating the logic model as a standard practice for the community school leadership team is also a powerful approach. The goal is for a wide swath of stakeholders to have "skin in the game" in school improvement, youth development, and enhanced learning opportunities.

Once created, this logic model should frame all conversations that happen among the collaborative leadership structures

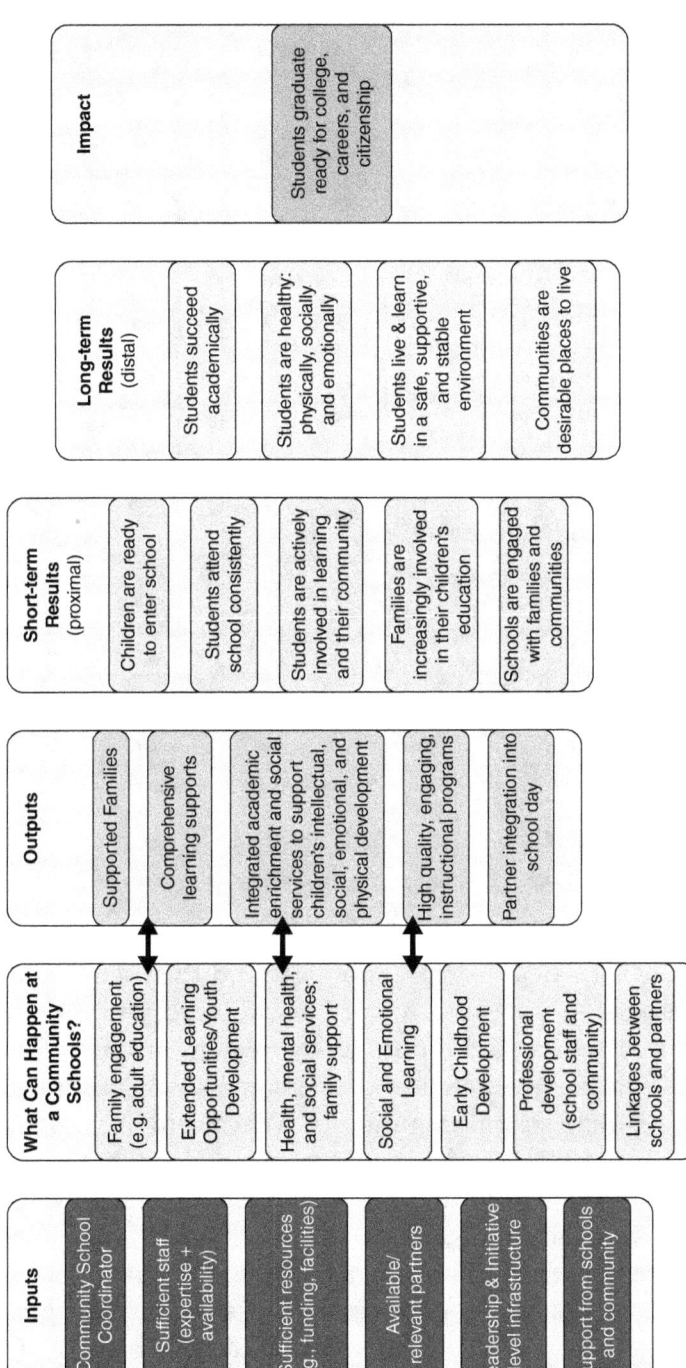

FIGURE 5.5 IEL Community School Logic Model

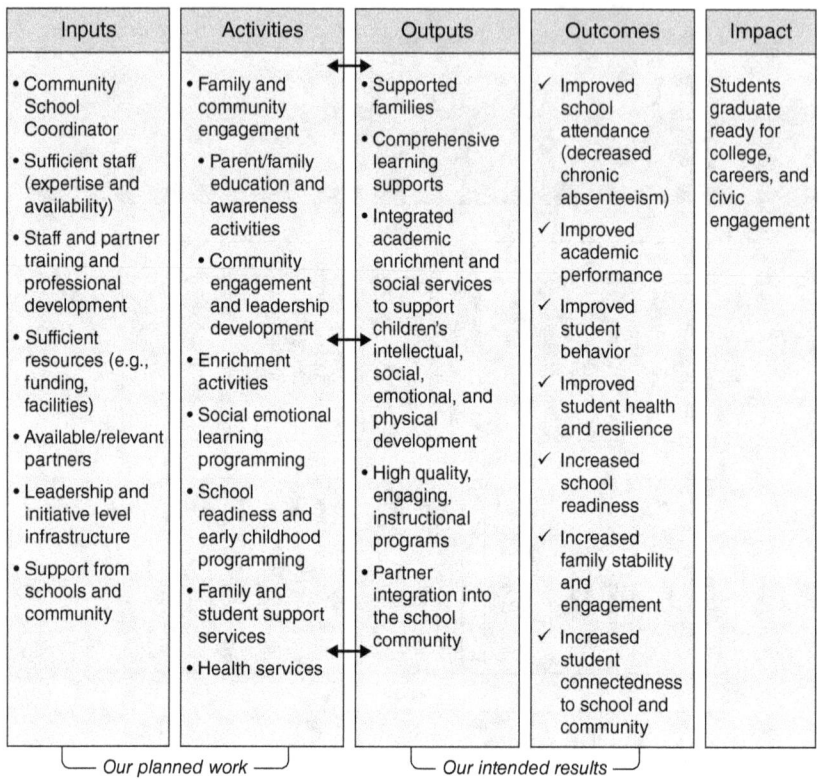

FIGURE 5.6 Fairfax County Community Schools Logic Model

described in Chapter 3. First, it can help set a baseline for the work to take place each school year and then serve as a guide for assessing progress toward each indicator. As Principal DeLarios Morán laid out above, when progress is made, gains can be celebrated and messaged to the entire internal and external school community. When progress is minimal or stalled, school staff, school teams, and partners can engage in strategic conversations to shift practice and develop new systems and solutions.

Here are examples of what several principals shared about the collaborative process of developing the logic model and its use by multiple stakeholders. Principal Queena Kim, (UCLA K-12 Community School, Los Angeles, CA) in

Building a Sound Foundation: Data, Evaluation, and Funding ♦ 105

FULL-SERVICE COMMUNITY SCHOOLS LOGIC MODEL

PROBLEM STATEMENT: Living in a lower-income rural area, and especially following 2+ years of both academic and socioemotional learning limitations due to the pandemic, students urgently need interventions to support their social and emotional wellness, safety, academic success, and career development

RESOURCES/INPUTS	STRATEGIES	OUTPUTS	SHORT-TERM OUTCOMES	LONG-TERM OUTCOMES	IMPACTS
Funding	**COLLABORATION** Align goals and resources to continuously improve sustainability to trauma mitigation supports	Parent, student & faculty surveys completed	5% more youths per year enjoy being in school (EYS 2023)	MTSS consistently, sustainably implemented with fidelity (TFI) School district staff interwoven in county-wide efforts (potential staff survey, possibly to combine with 21cclc staff survey)	Shared community-wide goals
Collaborations		MTSS teams implement CS/ARCH strategies	5% fewer youths per year at risk for lack of opportunities for prosocial involvement in the community (EYS 2027)	10% fewer youths at severe risk by 2027 (EYS 2027)	Routine of data-informed strategic planning
CS Coordinators in each project school	**ATTACHMENT** Build trust and connection with students and families thru support and engagement services	Pipeline services coordinated w/one another	Students arriving kindergarten-ready will increase by 10% each year (conducted in spring 2023, data to be analyzed this summer)	12% increase in funding dedicated to shared services by school districts by Sept. 2027	Districts have strong engagement skills to sustain youth and family involvement
CS Liaison		TFI conducted	80% of students in enrichment indicate it was helpful (SSOS spring 2023, data not yet available)	Increased protective factors, reduced risk factors (EYS 2027)	Students more connected to family, school, and community
Building Implementation Teams	**REGULATION (SELF)** Promote healthy coping, goal attainment, and self-efficacy	Community Circles conducted	Annual increase in % of students who can participate in activities they enjoy (EYS 2027)	Reduced rates of self-reported depression (EYS 2027)	Students have stronger self-regulation
Building Implementation Plans		Evidence-based drug prevention programming		Disconnected youth decrease 9% countywide to <5% by 2027 (DOL)	Students have greater post-secondary opportunities
MTSS Teams	**COMPETENCE** Use holistic learning to support academic success, post-secondary readiness, personal fulfillment	Anti-bullying, safe relationship programming	3% annual decrease in students reporting they are depressed most days (EYS 2023)	Eliminate disparities in suspensions (School Tool)	Youth are more resilient and less at-risk due to trauma
		MH First Aid trainings (youth, teen, adult)	3% annual increase in # of young people who would ask for help (EYS 2023)	Reduce youthful offenses (DCJS/local LE)	Students incorporate nutritious choices and physical activity into their lifelong wellness habits
	HEALTH Services and supports for active, healthy lifestyles are made accessible to youth and families	Wraparound teams		% of youths reading on grade level by 3rd grade will increase to an average of 75%+ by 2027 (NYSED Report Card)	Students make safer choices and are less at risk for sensation-seeking and impulsivity
		Co-located services/supports	5% annual decrease in youth chronically absent (School Tool)	% of youths earning a CDOS career pathway credential upon graduation will increase to 50% by 2027 (NYSED?)	Culture of identifying those at risk for mental health crisis, culture of asking for help
	(Pipeline services within the above: Health and wellness services, post-secondary and workforce readiness, high-quality learning in-and outside of school, early childhood	Literacy groups & Coffee chats	3% annual increase in students with 0 disciplinary referrals (School Tool)	% youths reporting physical activity 3+ days/week will increase 25% and the % of youths identified as obese will decrease 20% by Sept. 2027 (EYS 2027)	
		Basic needs access including telehealth, dental and food pantry	3% annual decrease in suspensions (School Tool)	% youths eating fruits and vegetables 2+ days/week will increase 25% and % of youths with nothing to eat at home will decrease by 50% by Sept. 2027 (EYS 2027)	
			5% annual decrease in impulsivity and sensation-seeking (EYS 2023)		

WAYNE COUNTY Community Schools

FIGURE 5.7 Wayne County Full-Service Community Schools Logic Model[10]

talked about how students can and should be involved in the process.

> Having students involved in data spaces has been really powerful. We have students on our School Site Council, which I don't think is always the case. We have also analyzed data together, and the students are the ones who are actually presenting the data and facilitating discussion with their teachers.

The community school coordinator, to whom we referred in the last chapter as "the glue," also plays a key role in interpreting and delivering school data to school staff. Former Principal Chuanika Sanders-Thomas (James Logan Elementary, Philadelphia, PA) affirmed the importance of maximizing the role of community school coordinator.

> You have to be intentional when setting up collaborative structures around data. Establishing a system where the community school coordinator is an integral part of the leadership team is essential. This ensures the coordinator stays informed about instruction, engages with the counseling department, and collaborates with other leadership team members. By fostering a space where everyone shares information and understands their role in community schools work, checking in with team members and evaluating progress effectively becomes much more manageable.

The community school coordinator is certainly the glue, linchpin, or connective tissue, especially with respect to their role on various school teams. The coordinator is also the one who spearheads the needs and assets assessment, ideally using logic model data to fuel the process. As Principal Mark Gaither (Wolfe Street Academy, Baltimore, MD) remarked:

> The evaluation of progress needs to assess both inputs and outputs. For example, how many parent meetings we are having (inputs) to how connected to the school

our parents are feeling (outputs), how many restorative conferences we are having (inputs) to how safe are students feeling in the school. What gets measured will be defined by the community assessments. If the community assessment shows a weakness in a given area and it is something inherent in the school's logic model, then the evaluation questions are: *What did you do about it?* And *What outcomes did you achieve?*

What Principal Gaither emphasized here speaks to evaluation in the context of the interconnected systems of community school strategies. Data is broader than assessing the impact of specific programs or interventions. It shows how all of the community school strategies, systems, and networks work together holistically to support students and the community at large.

Financing and Sustaining Your Community School

Now that we've talked about how to create a logic model and use it to gauge progress over time, we will now shift the focus to the funding of community schools. Throughout the following section, let's be sure to keep in mind that no two community schools are the same. All community schools operate within different contexts that influence the path to sustainable funding. Some districts may already have the support and political will of the mayor and superintendent, or perhaps even the state governor. There may already be nonprofits or community members advocating for or interested in championing community schools. Some districts may be on solid financial footing, or they may be facing budget shortfalls. Finally, changes in leadership (e.g. city or district) may result in more resources for community schools—or it may signal that resources may be allocated elsewhere.

When it comes to funding for community schools, a combination of several types of sources are involved: the local operating budget, state education funds, Federal Title funds, competitive federal grants, and private funding sources (see Figure 5.8).[11]

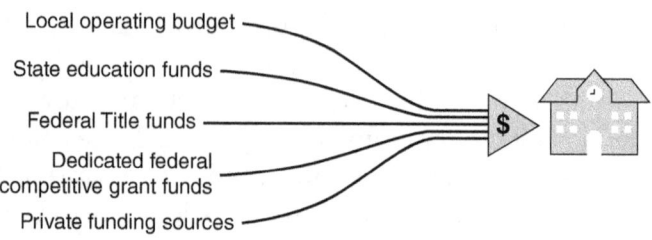

FIGURE 5.8 Funding Sources

Sharon Deich and Meghan Neary present a framework for growth and sustainability that includes three main types of actions for how to approach these different funding sources[12]:

1. Accessing and redeploying existing resources
2. Integrating and leveraging resources
3. Tapping into new resources

While each strategy is important on its own, the real strength is when all three are used in a coordinated approach.

Accessing and Redeploying Existing Resources

Most schools already have a base of funding to work with and expand the strategy. Mapping the current funding landscape across the five different funding categories in Figure 5.8 is a good place to start.

One of the likely core existing resources—federal funding programs—can support community schools through grants and allocations for areas such as physical and mental health care, career training, and family engagement. Most states already have funding streams dedicated to community schools or that can be reallocated, including in areas such as out-of-school time, comprehensive school improvement, and student supports. As explained in the book *Community Schools Revolution*,[13]

> Nearly every federal and state program focused on children, families, and communities can be integrated into the work of community schools. These include health and mental health services from Medicaid and the

federal Health Resources and Services Administration; food and nutrition assistance from the Department of Agriculture; community development monies from the Department of Housing and Urban Development; and restorative justice, violence prevention, and community safety funding from the Department of Justice.

When it comes to the local operating context, the immediate and actionable first step is to "map" the school budget. This process includes a thorough review of the budget against the school vision and the results of the needs and assets assessment. Listing budget items according to each key component can help identify the programs that are no longer aligned and where funds may be underutilized; it is this funding that can be reallocated to new strategies and programs. I want to underscore that eliminating programs and practices that are either misaligned or not producing the desired results is often the most challenging, but it is one of the most important exercises to undertake.

For state and local funding, there is an increasing number of free resources available through the US government and many of the national community school organizations, including periodic webinars about how to approach state and federal funding for community schools. The Learning Policy Institute (LPI) created a helpful document entitled, Federal Funding Sources for Community Schools that can be found on the LPI website. There are also two older, but still relevant sources. The first is a brief entitled Financing Community Schools: A Framework for Growth and Sustainability. This brief can be found on the Partnership for the Future of Learning's website. The second is a document called Financing Community Schools: Leveraging Resources to Support Student Success, easily accessible through a google search.

Integrating and Leveraging Resources

When it comes to integrating and leveraging resources, *braiding* and *blending* are words often cited. Both terms speak to the strategy of combining two or more sources of funding to support a given program or activity. Often, a combination of federal, state, and local streams, along with some private funding, can be woven together. What is the difference between blending and braiding? Braiding is when there are multiple funding streams, but each one is separately tracked and reported. Blending is a little easier—but also messier. The sources are co-mingled into a single pot, all in support of one purpose, and typically not tracked separately.

The community school coordinator and the Community School Leadership Team can work with district leaders to take inventory of existing funds and then investigate how an influx of new funds can be blended or braided in support of the school's vision and the results of the needs and assets assessment process.

An urban principal shared some recommendations:

> I would suggest setting up a series of meetings with your school's bookkeeper, the community school coordinator, and someone at the district/central office. The goal would be to gain in-depth knowledge of the ins and outs of different types of funding so that they know what to avoid, how to maximize those potential dollars, and understand the expectations that come with the braiding of funds. Here, the community school coordinator needs a seat at the table, and that invitation, nine times out of ten, needs to come from the principal.

A plan can then be developed to incorporate funding and resources from various partners that can lead to a more systemic and sustainable approach to your community school. Here, it might be helpful to recall the Essentials for Community School Transformation framework from Chapter 2 (see Figure 5.9).[14] This framework illustrates the most essential components of community schools and how the system functions as an integrated whole. More specifically, this diagram demonstrates the purpose of community schools, the drivers of the work, conditions that enable the work, and the six key practices. Finally, the outermost ring represents the broader supportive infrastructure that must be in place for school transformation.

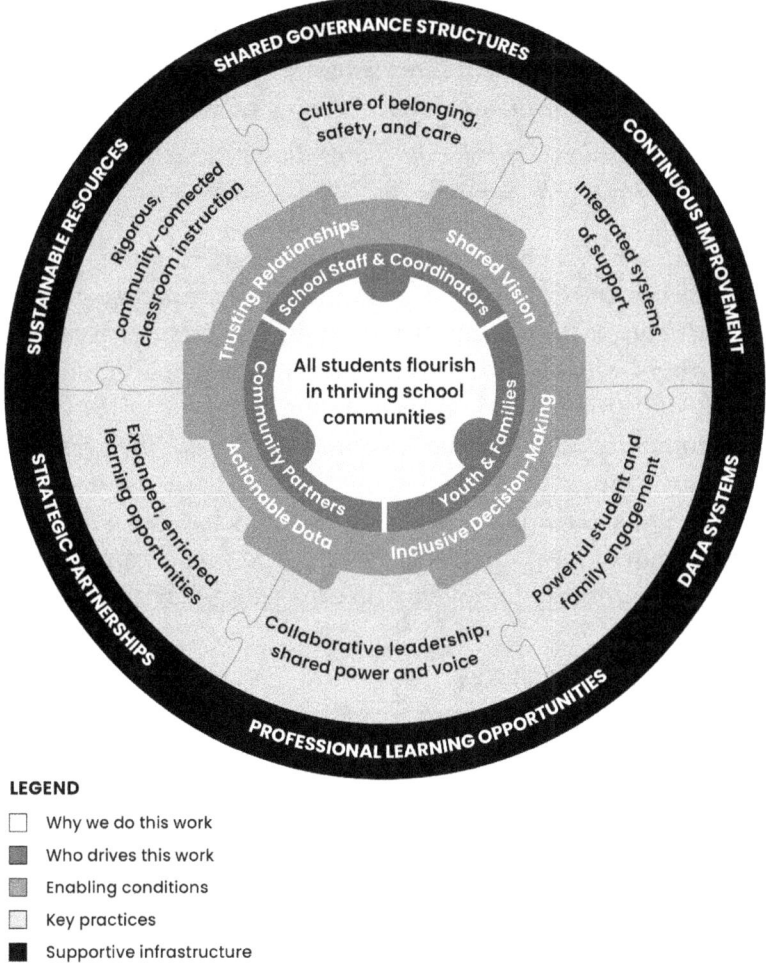

LEGEND
- ☐ Why we do this work
- ■ Who drives this work
- ▨ Enabling conditions
- ☐ Key practices
- ■ Supportive infrastructure

FIGURE 5.9 Community Schools Forward: Essentials for Community School Transformation

When it comes to supportive infrastructure, often partners can play a key role in securing additional education and non-education dollars. If your community school has a lead agency, this organization can often help think more expansively about integrated funding and bring some of their own funding sources to the table. The Community School Leadership Team and the Collaborative Partners Team discussed in Chapter 4 also can provide support, guidance, and legwork in terms of how funds are leveraged and integrated. When it comes to funding, working through all layers of the framework from the school all the way through local (and broader) governance structures is a necessity. One of my favorite ways of framing integrated funding through a community school lens comes from Jane Quinn, who presents a Thanksgiving analogy. As she explained,

> Traditionally, when schools think about funding, they think about a pie. The big question is *how are we going to slice it?* With community schools, the broader tent of partners allows us to think about the pie differently. The question is not just *how do we slice the pie we have*. It becomes, *how can we mobilize our assets to make it bigger?*

Principals are powerful agents of change within the microsystem of the school, and they can spearhead opportunities for their community to develop an ecosystem that does just this.

Tapping into New Resources

Finding new funding resources can happen in a number of ways. The Partnership for the Future of Learning brief, Financing Community Schools: A Framework for Growth and Sustainability, presents four different ways of creating new resources:[15]

- Solicit donations through in-kind and local fundraising
- Introduce public and private funders to community schools
- Research strategic priorities of local corporations, foundations, and community organizations to identify possible strategic alignment
- Work with community organizing groups to create, support, and promote funding for community schools

In Chapter 6, we will talk about how to advocate for funding, including creating an elevator pitch that can be used for each of these areas.

Securing Grant Funding

When it comes to grant-related funding, there is what Kristin McSwain, Senior Advisor and Director of the Office of Early Childhood, City of Boston, refers to as a hierarchy of grants. She views grants along a continuum, in terms of the simplest to the most cumbersome. The factors that can weigh a project down range from reporting requirements to other ongoing accountability structures. Funding from local neighborhood groups is often the most accessible option on the spectrum. This is typically the most comfortable avenue for school leaders to pursue. The next easiest would be grants from local philanthropic organizations. Next is the city or municipal grant, followed by the state grant. And then there is the federal grant—which often involves a heavy lift in terms of grant writing as well as required oversight. Two of the most common federal funding streams used by community schools are from the 21st Century Community Learning Centers Grant Program (supporting the implementation of academically enriching additional learning time that occurs outside of traditional school hours) and Full-Service Community Schools Grants Program (offering assistance for the planning, implementation, and management of community schools).

Although being awarded a federal grant can be a labor-intensive process, federal grants are worth writing and fighting for. They just require some soul-searching to determine whether the grant is a good fit for your school at this moment, considering what it provides versus the resources needed to complete the application and manage it. To ease the burden, many schools or districts bring in a consulting grant writer.

Yet, for some of these more cumbersome grants, funding does not just provide the resources to support a program or strategy; in fact, the grant becomes a convener, something that calls people together. As Jay Roscup explained,

> I would compare funding to a campfire, something that people gather around. The process of obtaining funding can be something that pulls people together. In

our district, there was a Safe Schools Healthy Students grant that really launched our work here. And the district failed, at least twice, trying to write that grant. But by the time it was obtained, they had been doing activity nights where the superintendent was baking cookies with the students and community volunteers were overseeing roller-skating, and they didn't wait to secure the funding to start trying some of the new initiatives. In fact, everyone started working together in different ways than they had before the grant-writing process started.

This idea of convening goes beyond the value of bonding and shared experiences. In fact, convening can involve partnering around a shared concern or sense of urgency. Schools may be able to collaborate with a trusted community-based organization (CBO) or nonprofit to apply for a grant together (perhaps the CBO has its own full-time or part-time grant writer), or they may be able to partner with another school. Several rural principals noted the power of partnering and sharing resources with other rural schools; for example, sharing a social worker across two schools. Other rural principals suggested the idea of approaching universities for support, "even if they are 50 miles away," one said.

A key lesson from the experience Jay Roscup shared is that some grants are worth writing even if they are not likely to be selected for funding. A planning group may want to ask, "If we spend one hundred hours on this project and it goes unfunded, will we still be closer to where we want to be?" In this way, undertaking a grant writing project can be a collaboration-building activity, a trust-building mechanism, an intensive visioning session, and a chance to think more deeply about the conditions for transformation. The opposite is also true. There may be grants that might be easier to obtain but not well aligned with your school's vision. For these grants, the school leader may have to make hard choices about whether they are worth pursuing. While most of the time funding does help, at times, depending on the strings that are attached, it can divert attention from what matters and even lead to confusion.

So how do you approach grant writing, whether it aims at diversifying or sustaining funding? One of the most important elements is being able to articulate an urgency around a school or community need—in other words, an issue that people cannot ignore and that presents a case that the audience cannot say no. This urgency is what's going to compel people to come together and take action. To start, the first soul searching question to ask is simple: "What *is* your urgency?"

For instance, the urgency might be equity, chronic absenteeism, or mental health. So, if you are a principal with a good understanding of the needs of your school, whether from listening or from the needs and assets assessment data, the next step is to think about the many layers of resources needed to address your urgency. Jay Roscup gives a helpful example about chronic absenteeism.

> For sure, you cannot ever prove direct causality. But what's the hunch about why kids aren't coming to school? It could be the need for childcare, it could be mental health, it could be physical health, it could be something like transportation. There are so many reasons why young people miss school. Are students feeling frustrated academically? Do we need to provide, socialization, support, social emotional learning groups or something of that nature? What are the issues and what are the programs or interventions that we need to make a difference?

Following this advice, if you're looking to decrease chronic absenteeism, you or your coordinator might explore out-of-school time or afterschool programs. Or perhaps you might look for a grant to provide a stipend for a staff member to monitor and address attendance. What's most important is to do your research and think entrepreneurially. There is some chance that the resources you need are somewhere in your vicinity, perhaps an organization whose funding guidelines align with your identified urgency. If you can coordinate and organize—in community school parlance—if you can get your coordinator, your Community School Leadership Team, and your school community to come together and rally, then it's possible a new partnership will be formed.

Here, the logic model discussed earlier may also come into play as a means of demonstrating how your school's strategies and programs are designed to achieve its goals. Many of the larger grants (including the federal government's Full-Service Community Schools Program referenced earlier in the chapter) require a logic model. Ideally, your logic model is easily transferable among grant programs. For example, if your district has applied for a Full-Service Community School grant, you may be able to use the same logic model for other grants, such as those for school safety or mental health. Again, the logic model is intended both to ground the work and articulate the measurable outcomes that are anchored in the community school strategies.

How to support your coordinator in the process of getting funding?

The principal, of course, is the chief advocate for their building. Even if the coordinator is the one who spearheads the grant-writing process, the principal's presence, buy in, and commitment must be felt throughout the entire process.

Principals may want to provide coaching for their coordinators, especially when building their capacity to take greater ownership of this process. As such, principals should keep the following considerations in mind:

- ♦ Create the time and space for the coordinator to go after these grants. Make sure there is some relief for day-to-day responsibilities so that the coordinator can explore options and do the necessary grunt work.
- ♦ Encourage the coordinator to be proactive and relentless. Even if odds seem unlikely, the coordinator should keep their ear on the ground, listen as much as possible, and keep sharing the urgency with different stakeholders.
- ♦ Be open to giving your coordinator permission to share different types of data, even data you might not be proud of. Even if the data feels like it might paint the school in a negative light, *this* is what shows the urgency. Don't shy away from using it.

Additional coaching points to consider are as follows:

- Partner with those who might make the process less overwhelming, whether it's a local nonprofit, a lead agency, or a community advocate.
- Consider outreach to all different types of community resources. Figure 5.2 from the previous chapter, laying out a range of community resources that could be part of a collaborative, could be a good place to start.
- Don't be afraid to approach local foundations. Often foundations are open to having conversations about urgent issues, especially when they are aligned to the local foundation's mission.
- Check to see whether there is a United Way in your region that might be interested in collaborating. United Ways have been supportive of and even spearheaded major community school initiatives across the country.
- Learn from unsuccessful efforts. If a grant was not accepted, listen to the grant reviews and learn from what was missing. If a local organization is not interested in funding, ask for feedback regarding what you might do differently the next time.
- Shoot for multiple-year grants, even if small scale. You want to set up systems for longer-term success—which of course takes time and sustained funding.
- Encourage a diverse compilation of grants. Ideally, you want to have layered funding so that if one funding source dries up or ends unexpectedly, your programming and strategies can sustain the blow.

Responses from Principals in the Field

What data are you using? How are you looking behind the data? What's the "why"?

There will always be traditional standardized data points, such as math, reading, and English language proficiency scores. But in community schools, we are diving deep into data about the students themselves. And instead of saying that we know what everyone needs, we ask them questions directly. One way of doing this is by conducting our own surveys for students, asking: *Are your teachers supporting you? Do you feel like you have a person who is supporting you in the school? Do you feel successful in the school?* We then present this data to teachers in faculty meetings. We also did an "envisioning your school" session with parents and then shared that data with staff and families. Ultimately, we need to find out whether what we are doing is gaining traction. How are parents, families, and staff working together to get closer to achievement goals? If we don't connect and look more broadly at student achievement, we miss things.

Anthony Frye, *Washington S.T.E.M. Elementary School, Lynn, MA*

The difference in how data is looked at in community schools lies in the depth, flexibility, and inclusivity of the approach. Community schools use data not just to track academic performance, but to foster a rich, responsive learning environment that includes the entire community in the process. Interdisciplinary teams, through the work of a community school coordinator, regularly review data to prioritize resources and prepare individualized plans to make sure all students get the opportunities and support they need. The goal is to support all aspects of student development, from academic, social, and emotional, and to use data sets in these areas to guide decisions that make the school a more integrated part of the local community—and vice-versa.

Richard M. Gordon IV, *Assistant Superintendent, School District of Philadelphia, and former Principal of Paul Robeson High School, Philadelphia, PA*

Our academic data is where we always start. We also have goals within the Florida model of community schools, including healthcare access and volunteer and engagement goals. But we need to look at both sides and where the intersections are.

Chronic absenteeism has been a real problem since Covid. With chronic absenteeism, the "why" is still linked to unmet needs in the family—the kids are seldom just playing hooky. We need to look deeply at the data for root causes. What's really at the core of this problem? And how many other families are affected by the same issues? When you get down to the root cause, it allows you to be able to fix the real problems. Our goal as a community school is more than about kids getting grade level skills—it is about addressing root causes to ensure that kids will be able to function as successful adults.

Bethany Groves, *Principal at Webster Elementary, St. Augustine, Florida*

This chapter emphasized the importance of securing diverse and sustainable funding for community schools. Building on that foundation, the next chapter will explore the principal's critical role in advocating for the policies and resources needed to fully realize their community school vision. This shift in focus highlights that financial stability is merely the first step in creating successful community schools; principals must think beyond managing budgets and become active champions for their schools, influencing decision-making at various levels to ensure their community schools have the support they need to succeed.

Notes

1 Phillips, M., Brooks-Gunn, J., Duncan, G. J., Klebanov, P., & Crane, J. (1998). Family background, parenting practices, and the black-white test score gap. In C. Jencks & M. Phillips (Eds.), *The black-white test score gap* (pp. 103–145). Washington, DC: Brookings Institution Press; see also Rothstein, R. (2010, October 14). *How to fix our schools* (Issue Brief #286). Washington, D.C.: Economic Policy Institute. Retrieved from www.epi.org/publication/ib286/0

2 DeWitt, P. (2011). The issue of school climate: A conversation with Jonathan Cohen. *Education Week*. Retrieved from https://www.edweek.org/education/opinion-the-issue-of-school-climate-a-conversation-with-jonathan-cohen/2011/11

3   Lubell, E. (2011). *Building community schools: A guide for action*. New York, NY: Children's Aid Society. This specific graphic was developed by the Coalition for Community Schools, an initiative of the Institute for Educational Leadership (IEL)
4   This section, including the figures, draws from the following document: Kellogg Foundation (2001). *Logic model development guide: Logic models to bring together planning, evaluation & action*. Battle Creek, MI: W.K. Kellogg Foundation.
5   *Logic Models: A beginner's guide*. Retrieved from https://www.michigan.gov/-/media/Project/Websites/leo/Folder20/Developing_a_Logic_Model_Guidex.pdf?rev=d4c120d3afc248e98404450806b4db30
6   Family and Youth Services Bureau. (n.d.). *Logic model tip sheet*. Retrieved from https://www.acf.hhs.gov/sites/default/files/documents/prep-logic-model-ts_0.pdf
7   IEL. (n.d.). *Community schools logic model*. Retrieved from https://www.nyscommunityschools.org/wp-content/uploads/2019/01/F8-logic-model.pdf
8   Fairfax County Community Schools Logic Model. (2023). Retrieved from https://www.fairfaxcounty.gov/health-humanservices/sites/health-humanservices/files/Assets/Documents/SCYPT/CSFC%20Implementation%20Framework%20-%20Clean%20Copy%20%2810.23%29%20%281%29.pdf
9   Wayne County Community Schools. (2024). *Full service community schools logic model*. Retrieved from https://drive.google.com/file/d/1WNjv3seE2AnEouYcBhGOaQ6VaPrxJKfh/view?usp=sharing
10 Wayne County Community Schools. (2024). Full service community schools logic model. Retrieved from https://drive.google.com/file/d/1WNjv3seE2AnEouYcBhGOaQ6VaPrxJKfh/view?usp=sharing
11 Okogbue, O., Sanders, M., Angeles-Figueroa, A., & Sacks, V. (2022). *Recent funding approaches and sources for community schools*. Retrieved from https://www.childtrends.org/publications/recent-funding-approaches-and-sources-for-community-schools
12 Deich, S. & Neary, M. (2020). *Financing community schools: A Framework for Growth and Sustainability*. Retrieved from https://futureforlearning.org/2020/04/16/financing-community-schools/
13 Blank, M., Harkavy, I., Quinn, J., Villarreal, L., & Goodman, D. (2023). *The community schools* revolution. Retrieved from https://www.

communityschoolsrevolution.org/going-big-big-apple-how-grassroots-movement-helped-launch-nation-s-largest-citywide-community, p. 20.
14 Community schools forward. (2023). *Framework: Essentials for community school transformation.* Retrieved from https://learningpolicyinstitute.org/project/community-schools-forward
15 Deich, S. & Neary, M. (2020). *Financing community schools: A Framework for Growth and* Sustainability. Retrieved from https://futureforlearning.org/2020/04/16/financing-community-schools/, p. 14

6

The Principal's Role in Advocating for Change

Introduction

The previous chapter focused on using data internally—to improve the teaching and learning inside the school, meet the needs of the community, and drive a cycle of continuous improvement. We also talked about how to support the coordinator in working with local partners and businesses in the community to secure funding.

Now, let's build on the last chapter's discussion of data, funding, and resource recruitment by focusing on this question: How do you make the case for your school district, city, and possibly even your state to support your community school? If the work of the previous chapters seems like more than enough right now, consider bookmarking this chapter for later in your community school development.

Data for Advocacy

When making the case for funding or resources for your community school, it's important to be clear about what you need and why you need it. Let's start with the "what" first. Here is a list to use as a starting point.

You might need funding/support for:

1. The community school coordinator position: You may be looking to secure temporary funding for a community school coordinator and/or ensure longer term, sustainable funding for the coordinator position
2. Additional partnerships aligned with data from the needs and assets assessment
3. Technical assistance for different constituent groups (principals and school leaders, coordinators, teachers, district leaders, and district staff) about how to implement community school strategies more effectively within their given roles
4. Sending a team from your school to community school conferences or to visit an exemplary community school
5. Community school professional development through a national community school network such as the National Center for Community Schools, the Institute for Educational Leadership, or a regional technical assistance center

New policies, including:

1. Professionalization, elevation, and institutionalization of the coordinator position
2. Line items in district, city, or state budgets for the coordinator position
3. An office for community schools within the district that is recognized as a critical component of teaching and learning, not buried within the district's organizational chart
4. Ways to ensure ease of service delivery, maximize the use of out-of-school time, and/or how to create smooth pathways for different agencies and sectors to work together
5. The redirection of existing city or state grants, e.g. neighborhood safety initiatives or after-school programs, so the money becomes part of the community school budget

6. Establishing procedures for hiring principals and teachers with a community school background and/or mindset
7. Board policy affirming that partners aligned with schools' needs are welcomed and appreciated

Whatever it is that you are advocating for, you first need to consider how to make the case to your district, city, or state. In other words, once you are clear on the "what," you can then focus on defining the "why." Why should your district, city, or state care about your school or listen to the argument you are trying to make? How can you use data so that policy leaders feel compelled to change existing practices or structures to support your community school?

The first step to answering those questions is to determine what data you have to work with and, of that data, what is most compelling. The second step is to create a succinct narrative, often called an elevator pitch. These are the building blocks you can use to create the sense of "urgency" discussed in the last chapter.

What data is most effective and in what form?

The answer to this question likely depends on where you are on your community school journey, how long you've been a community school (if at all), and what data you have been able to collect thus far. In some cases, you may already have some quantitative data that shows improvement in short-term metrics, such as the ones described in the previous chapter, including:

- Chronic absenteeism
- Disciplinary incidents
- Student and family sense of belonging
- Family attendance at school-wide events
- Parents participating in school decision-making
- Access to health care
- School climate and culture
- Access to out-of-school programming
- Access to mental health support

You may even have some longer term data that shows improvement in categories such as:

- Graduation rates
- Drop-out rates
- On-time grade promotion rates
- Standardized test scores
- Family mobility rates
- Juvenile crime[1]

However, if you are still in the early stages of building your initiative, you may not have any data yet. In that case, all hope is not lost. In fact, you can gather data from other promising community schools to show what is possible for your own school context. In other words, even without your own data, you can make the case that community schools are a research-backed approach to improving outcomes for students and communities. As Mark Gaither, principal of Wolfe Street Academy, Baltimore, MD, explained, grounding your data in the national movement is a sign of strength.

> Connecting the work at your school to what came before and what already exists is a critical part of advocacy. Trying to separate yourself out too much from national, local, or even other schools diminishes what can be done. Showing how you are an extension of the good work others are doing gives you more allies, more power, and more stories to show what could be possible. It also helps you from having to recreate the wheel every time.

There is considerable research on community schools from which to draw. Return on investment (ROI) data, measuring how much is earned (the profit) in comparison to the amount of money spent on an investment, can be particularly compelling. Another way to view these studies is that they document the relationship of costs to benefits. As discussed in Chapter 1, a 2013 study conducted by the Finance Project, a 2012 study performed by Economic Modeling Specialists Inc., and a

2019 study commissioned by the ABC Community School partnership in Albuquerque, found that for every $1 invested in student supports at community schools, the community school coordinator position itself, and other types of community school programming yielded between a $7%–$14% return on investment.[2] When it comes to the community school coordinator specifically, the 2019 ABC Community School Partnership study showed that each dollar invested in the coordinator generated a return of approximately $7, due in part to the funding resources the coordinator was able to generate.[3] This study demonstrates that the community school coordinator position yields a significant return on the original monetary investment and can be a powerful advocacy tool.

The following two studies (also discussed briefly in Chapter 1) likewise help provide persuasive data. The landmark 2017 Learning Policy Institute and National Education Policy Center study[4] synthesized findings from 143 rigorous community school evaluations. It found that well-implemented community schools are successful at reducing barriers to learning and lead to better academic outcomes—especially with low-income students who attend high-poverty schools.[5] Another important study, led by the RAND Corporation, looked at community schools in New York City—the largest community school initiative in the country. It found improved student attendance in all grades, a positive impact on high school students' graduation, and a reduction of disciplinary incidents for elementary and middle school students. It also showed a more positive school climate and culture in elementary and middle school. Finally, it revealed a positive impact on math achievement and on the credits accumulated by high school students.

In terms of a more specific example at the local level, in Austin, Texas, five years after adopting the community school strategy, both a middle school and high school saw significant gains. In fact, Webb Middle School became the highest performing Title I Middle School in Austin. Similarly, after five years, Regan High School doubled enrollment and partnered with a local community college to start an early college program that enabled many of its students to earn associate degree credits. In addition, they improved the graduation rate from 50% to 85%.[6]

If more rural examples are a better fit for your community, a partnership with Tennessee Governor Bill Lee and the community school organization *Communities in Schools* enabled access to community school resources for 11,000 students who attended rural schools. As a result, 82% of these students showed improvements in attendance, 94% matriculated to their next grade, and 97% of seniors graduated from high school.[7]

Do not underestimate the power of qualitative data and storytelling, be it from your own district or an already established district.

> At Gibsonton Elementary School, just south of Tampa, Florida, there was an unsolved mystery around why so many students were arriving late to school on a daily basis. Their community school coordinator started asking families why their children were late so often. She heard from parents that it was so dark in the morning that they often waited until the sun came up to leave for school. When the coordinator pressed the parents on what was happening, they said that there were no streetlights, and kids were walking in the middle of the road to school. At that point, the coordinator then got in her car and traced some of the main paths to school. What she realized was that not only were there no streetlights, but there were also no sidewalks. In fact, kids were walking to school in the middle of the road in full darkness. As a result of the coordinator's findings, over 50 streetlights were soon installed, along with sidewalks along the main roads (and some side streets) leading to school. Now, the majority of Gibsonton students attend school on time. As the coordinator explained, "If we didn't listen to the voices of parents and asked the questions that needed to be asked, we wouldn't know… and we would continue to wonder why these students keep coming to school so late."[8]

By the time this book is published, there will be a much greater sampling of data from which to draw. Don't be afraid to reach out to other principals for their success stories or look online for school data reports or other measurements of community schools' successes. As Principal Gaither said earlier, showing how your school is an extension of the good work others are doing can be a powerful tool in making the case for what is possible in your school and surrounding community.

As we discussed in Chapter 4, many of those entrenched in the world of community schools view the community school coordinator (CSC) as one of the two most essential components of a community school initiative. As the Gibsonton Elementary School story above shows, ensuring that a school has a coordinator who is positioned in the organizational chart as a school leader, serving as a key partner to the principal and "ambassador to the entire school staff and outside community," is one of the most important "asks" you can make when it comes to advocating for your school.

Ensuring a Full-Time Community School Coordinator

Principal Mark Gaither, a multi-decade community school principal, played a significant role in the advocacy leading to Baltimore's 2016 community school policy. As he shared,

> I'd go so far as to say that opening up a school without a coordinator would be as ridiculous opening up a school without a principal. This is where the notion of an advocacy team comes in. What you are seeking is the support of the broadest possible number of humans, a city full of voters who believe, in their emotional selves, that their child, or their neighborhood school (think property values!) deserves a community school coordinator. Advocacy is about winning hearts and minds.

When it comes to funding for a coordinator, principals may want to revisit the three main types of actions suggested in the framework for growth and sustainability presented in Chapter 5[9]: (1) accessing and deploying existing resources, (2) integrating and leveraging resources, and (3) tapping into new resources.

To start, are there any existing resources that might be available? From the mapping work we discussed in the previous chapter, are there any areas where funds are already allocated but could be redirected to support a coordinator role? Are there funding streams that fail to achieve the desired effects that can be reallocated to this position?

With respect to integrating and leveraging resources, there may be partners your school already has in place (e.g. local nonprofits or city agencies) that may be willing to contribute to covering a portion of the position's costs.[10] Also, this may be an opportunity to partner with nearby schools or districts to co-fund a coordinator who works across multiple sites. While the most effective ratio is to have one coordinator for each school, often more rural districts have seen success with having a County Office of Education hire a coordinator to enhance access and foster connections, particularly with other County agencies.[11]

In terms of tapping into new resources, one option is to look to the philanthropic community. Local foundations are often supportive of community schools and might be willing to support a community school coordinator position, or even help a school catalyze a position (i.e. the foundation funds 100% the first year, 75% the second year, 50% the third year, and so on). Each year, the school gradually assumes more of the cost until it is paying for the position in its entirety.

In addition, it may make sense to see whether federal 21st Century Community Learning Centers (21st CCLC) grants might be a fit. These grants, designed to support out-of-school time programming, are used by many existing community schools to underwrite coordinators' salaries. As of 2024, federal funding for 21st CCLC grants totals $1.3 billion.[12]

Once you determine the data available to you (whether specific to your school or from other exemplary community schools) that can justify the "what" of your ask, the next step is to figure out how to communicate your request.

How to Craft an Elevator Pitch

The communications vehicle needs to be succinct enough to keep the audience engaged. It needs to be inviting and inclusive. It needs to be persuasive. Most of all, it needs to matter to people.

Your elevator pitch is a short "call to action" that doesn't take more than an elevator ride to deliver. An elevator pitch is designed to support any formal opportunity you have to broadcast what your community school has done well, why potential supporters should get behind you, and how they might engage in the work. For those less formal opportunities, you may want to think of this as a "cocktail party pitch," in which you find yourself talking about your community school in a more casual setting, trying to gain an ally and/or spread the good word.

Whatever you decide to call it, this pitch in a community school context needs to do two things. First, it needs to create the sense of urgency that we talked about in the last chapter—raising an issue that people cannot ignore—to which they are compelled to respond. Here, it is important to put in some legwork to better know your audience. What is important, right now, to your potential supporters? What urgency will align with their current priorities? What are they most focused on? Second, this pitch needs to clearly articulate what a community school is. While community schools and community school strategies are comprehensive, the language in an elevator pitch must be simple.

While there are many ways of structuring an elevator pitch, here is a loosely adapted template from San Diego Unified School District's website, that was previously created for community schools[13].

> *Urgency* (10–15 seconds): Grab attention by articulating the urgency. What is needed—for example, decreasing chronic absenteeism or addressing a recent uptick of violence in the community—and why is it so important?
>
> *Introduction* (30 seconds): What does it mean to be a community school and what is special about your school? As we've discussed throughout the book, community schools

can be hard to describe with minimal words. It may make sense to use language that others have crafted. This definition, offered in Chapter 2 (alongside others), is one of many starting points that might be helpful:

> The community schools strategy transforms a school into a place where educators, local community members, families, and students work together to strengthen conditions for student learning and healthy development. As partners, they organize in- and out-of-school resources, supports, and opportunities so that young people thrive.[14]

Addressing the urgency (1 minute): How does your community school specifically address the urgent problem? What data can you share that will illustrate either your progress thus far or what other community schools have been able to accomplish?

Wrap up (15–20 seconds): Why should your audience engage and how, specifically, can they support you? What are you asking for?

Your elevator pitch may be the only pitch you end up giving, it may precede a longer presentation, or it may serve as the framework for a more robust presentation.

With this format in mind, let's now turn to the "who." "Who" or "whom" (as the case may be) might you want to approach as a potential funder or supporter of your community school? Who is the right audience for this pitch? Possible recipients might be the school committee or school board; district, city, or state leaders and legislators; city and state agencies, such as health and human services or housing; local nonprofits or foundations; or even a local reporter.

Another question to ask is "who" delivers the elevator pitch? The answer depends on the audience and the purpose. But as many principals and coordinators expressed, when students and families involved in community school initiatives lend their voices to help make the case, it often carries the most weight of all.

For a great resource on tailoring your elevator pitch and messaging to a bi-partisan audience (or to a partisan audience, if it fits your context), see Appendix D for some key messages excerpted from the Coalition for Community Schools' *Community Schools Communications Toolkit*.

We are now going to turn to what happens when the "who" becomes much broader; in other words, what happens, and what is possible, when individual groups (e.g. local nonprofits) decide that they are fully committed to community schools and are ready to unite in their advocacy efforts.

Creating a Broad Advocacy Team

The following two short case studies focus on how broad swaths of advocates rallied together to either launch or sustain their local community school initiatives. I share them here in the hope that these stories might serve as inspiration to think about your communities, and the potential for mobilizing your communal resources, in a different light.

The New York City Story[15]

While seemingly political, this story is really about advocacy and coalition building.

In 2012, prior to New York City's mayoral election, community organizers prepared and developed a platform for the candidates, representing and incorporating the many voices and concerns of community members. The organizers' goal was to ensure that the incoming mayor, whoever it may be, implemented reforms that the community *itself* wanted for students and families. This "Education Roadmap," which became known as PS 2013, included community schools as one of its recommendations.

At this point, the advocacy mission to sway the mayoral candidates began in earnest. The major teachers union in New York arranged field trips for candidates to visit exemplary community schools in New York City and Cincinnati. Local activists, coordinated by the Coalition for Educational Justice, conducted

75 community meetings that brought together superintendents, parents, students, teachers, and champions within the community. Most colorfully, the activists commandeered a bus (that they painted in a bright blue to attract attention as it traveled through the city) to park in front of the mayoral campaign events. Inside the bus, seats had been removed. As described in the book *The Community Schools Revolution*,

> Members of the public were welcome to come inside… [where] they would find clear buckets labeled with different education issues, such as art and music, better food, physical education, or more robust social services. People could vote on their priorities by placing a piece of paper in one or more of the buckets… You could see in real time what people wanted in their schools… in [which] were things that are core tenets of community schools.[16]

When Mayor Bill de Blasio was elected, he stood behind this roadmap, initiated and promoted by the community, and promised to launch 100 community schools in his first term (Office of the Mayor, n.d.). Today, community schools are thriving in New York City. As of 2022–2023, there are over 400 community schools in New York City, across every school district. These schools are funded through a combination of city, state, and federal public resources, supplemented by private sources.[17]

The Baltimore Story

My own research in Baltimore uncovered another remarkable example of how community and coalitions were central to generating support for community schools, and ultimately for funding and policy adoption.[18] For many years (especially the period from 2008 to 2016), city and district support for community schools was tenuous at best. Whether community schools would survive year to year was a constant source of concern.

Community activists' antennae were raised when one of the mayoral candidates (who then became mayor) publicly pledged a $10 million commitment to funding afterschool programs, which, the way community schools worked in Baltimore, fed directly into community school funding. However, year after year, the mayor's budget didn't reflect this pledge. The community (including parents, students, teachers, and grassroots organizations) sprang into action, rallying to ensure that the mayor followed through on this original commitment and kept the movement afloat. Each time the mayor threatened to cut funding for out-of-school time, organizing groups banded together to put the pressure on policy makers that ultimately secured the promised funding. In fact, at one Baltimore City Council's Taxpayer's Night in 2008, there were over 800 people who showed up to support community schools.

One of the participants in my study talked about the building of "infrastructure that nobody ever saw ... that was happening in coffee shops, late-night meetings, and early morning phone calls. All of this is incredibly important to the story of Baltimore. If it had been a top-down effort, it would never have been successful because community schools have always recognized and empowered community in a way that was very different."[19]

Organizations that supported community schools united in a number of ways to show their support. Previously existing coalitions within the city came together, with the goal of getting the attention of policy leaders and maximizing their individual coalition impact. In addition, there were a number of times in which the nonprofit partners supporting schools aligned to make the case for more community schools and additional community school funding. One participant in my study explained that several lead community-based agencies were "amazing organizers ... and that it was literally how they did business." These efforts resulted in the City of Baltimore adopting a Community School Policy in 2016. As of 2024, 97% of schools in Baltimore are community schools.[20]

My research reinforced the impact of advocacy and pressure on political leaders by individuals, community-based organizations, and coalitions who, themselves, had benefited from the model, saw its value, and had a meaningful voice in informing what the initiative looked like in their communities. In layman's terms, do not underestimate the power of what happens when communities join forces to articulate what community schools are and to advocate for more support.

Community School Champions

When trying to determine who should be a part of the advocacy team, one of the most essential questions is the following: *Who are the champions here?* In other words, who are the individuals who are most passionate about community schools? Or, are there people who, with some gentle nudging, might realize that there is great alignment of their goals and those of your community school? Individuals to consider as champions may include nonprofit leaders, other principals, teachers, community leaders, district and city leaders, local philanthropists, faith-based leaders, parents, and really, anyone who could be considered a potential champion. It is also possible that champions exist who do not know about the work underway at your school and the existing momentum, and they might be excited about collaborating and learning more. Ask parents and non-profit leaders to suggest others who are passionate about education about education.

So, what role does the principal play when it comes to finding champions? Much of it comes down to the relationship between the coordinator and the principal and the way that responsibilities have been delineated at your school. As we discussed in Chapter 4, in a healthy principal/coordinator relationship, the coordinator can take many responsibilities off the principal's plate. Chris Battaglia, former Principal at Ben Franklin High School, Baltimore, MD, shared insights on responsibilities in and outside the school. As he explained,

> The best relationship between the principal and the coordinator is one where the coordinator operates as the "principal of all things NOT the school." This means, the coordinator understands the vision of the principal and has their trust to speak on behalf of the school. As

a result, when outside agencies see or hear the principal trusting the coordinator, advocacy can spread faster and more broadly because it does not get bottlenecked waiting for meetings with the principal.

The school principal must work hand-in-hand with the coordinator to champion community schools to various audiences, such as neighborhood associations, school committees, potential funders, and elected officials. The coordinator often acts as the conduit.

Dante DeTablan, Principal Battaglia's former coordinator, provided his perspective on the advocacy work. As he noted,

> I organized our school community in participating in advocacy efforts, e.g., filling the school buses with parents, students, teachers, and community partners and traveled to Annapolis during our campaigns. I also helped with providing the data as we testified to legislators at our city hall (and in Annapolis and Washington, D.C.!) and built relationships with them. Of course, I kept Chris, our principal, updated with all the activities and encouraged him to participate as he deemed appropriate.

Principals and coordinators may wish to divide the labor in terms of how they bring advocates and champions together to talk about the mission of their community school and the value of community schools writ large. But ultimately, the principal owns the work. When a principal reaches out and says, "my students need your support," it's a powerful voice. You can capitalize on the inherent respect for the role—everyone growing up knew the principal in their school as the authority—so your voice can rally people together.

Mark Gaither, who we heard from earlier in the chapter, sums it up perfectly.

> The call to action that I frequently fall back upon is the idea that finally, FINALLY, we have the tool we need to make a real change. Now is the time. Don't let it go

by. I call upon folks to realize that we have known for years how to educate children. We have known how to prevent discipline issues and suspensions. The question has not been one of trying to figure out how to do it. The question has always been whether or not we (and that is the collective "we" composed of voters, politicians, and citizens) have the will to do what we know works. The challenge, the call, is to say to people, "We know what works. We have the tools. Will you get on board and make it happen?"

We all know that creating the capacity for the principal to spend their limited time thinking about the "goings on" outside of the school building is a herculean task—even with the support of an amazing community school coordinator. However, community school principals have an authentic role to play in encouraging the community, district, and state to do more to support them. The call to action is about creating awareness, building on momentum, and highlighting the great work of their schools so that more and more stakeholders want to join the movement and do their part to advance it.

⁇ Responses from Principals in the Field

Do you have an example of an effective elevator pitch or can you share a time you successfully made a pitch for your community school?

Our district has reached a crisis in chronic absenteeism with 21% of elementary students and 36% of secondary students missing over 17 days of instruction per year. The consequences of chronic absenteeism are devastating once students reach high school. Union has a goal to have 100% students graduate college and career-ready! As a community school, we seek to understand the needs of our students, families and community. We know 57% of our students go to college. The construction, aviation and medical academies were recently created to ensure our students have the skills to be successful in our community, whether they attend college or a career path. We have developed four pathways based upon our community needs assessments from students, families and the community. You can help by providing funding, mentors, or experiences for students before, during, or after school hours. We know when students see relevance and experience a sense of belonging, their attendance and academic outcomes increase.

Theresa Kiger, *Former Principal Roy Clark Elementary, Tulsa, Oklahoma and current Executive Director of Elementary Education for Union Public Schools, Tulsa, OK*

First, in Florida, we call our community schools "Community Partnership Schools." For our school, we have a number of steps that we use to build a strong, data-driven case. We start the process by identifying key metrics. What data points are most relevant to us? This could include student performance metrics, attendance rates, graduation rates, and socio-economic indicators. We then conduct our needs assessment, breaking down the data to highlight disparities and areas needing improvement. This can help in pinpointing where some of our partnerships could have the most impact. When it comes to advocacy, we do two things—we highlight success stories and use case studies from other community partnership schools to show potential benefits. We present these stories and our specific data to stakeholders, including parents, community leaders, and potential partners—and we always use visual aids like charts and graphs to make the data more accessible and compelling. Once we identify our key partners, we develop a logic model that outlines how our partnership will address identified needs and lead to desired outcomes. And the last step, which is ongoing, is to monitor and adjust, continuously collecting and analyzing data to monitor progress and make necessary adjustments to strategies and programs.

Pio Rizzo, *Principal at Gulfside Elementary, Holiday, Florida*

From the start, we educated our Board of Education about the benefits of the community schools strategy. We regularly informed them about our community school efforts and their impact on our students, school, families, and community.

One of the first things we did was invite our board members to come to our schools and attend events as much as possible. At each board meeting, we would review a schedule of upcoming functions, and members would sign up for the events they could attend. We would recognize them at the events whenever possible so family members and students could acknowledge and interact with them. Board members had opportunities to interface with all members of our community—not just the most visible ones. They began to see that there were families we needed to reach and resources to provide.

When we had opportunities to present to the Board, we always started with data. We'd present the data identifying how many students were proficient and where the gaps were. We then showed evidence of the community schools work we'd started and celebrated successes. They would also see where community schools strategies were built into our strategic plan. We'd reinforce that the community schools strategy provides opportunities to develop authentic partnerships with families and community agencies to offer support identified through our needs and opportunities assessment process to move all our students to success. They could then advocate for community schools and relate this information to our community.

We would also partner with local organizations to help meet the needs of our families and students. We'd turn to the Rotary for funds to support community schools initiatives. One of our local churches provided snacks and hygiene bags for our unaccompanied youth. Another church across the street from our main campus gave our families access to their food bank. Mothers and Babies supported our early childhood initiative (birth through kindergarten). A local hospital provided a dental van, and we requested they come more often and expand to our preschools. Overall, we'd integrate resources our community partners could provide and let them know how they fit into our strategic plan to improve student success. We would also show them how their support was making a difference. In return, word spread about our work, and other agencies would contact us to collaborate by providing different services and grant opportunities.

Patricia Follette, *former Superintendent of Schools, Whitney Point Central School District, NY*

By developing and employing an elevator pitch to garner resources and support and then bringing the community together around common goals and successes, community school leaders can create the conditions for equitable outcomes for all students, a topic explored more deeply in the next chapter.

Notes

1. Coalition for Community Schools. (n.d.). *Community schools: Promoting student success, a rationale and results framework.* Retrieved from https://www.communityschools.org/wp-content/uploads/sites/2/2021/01/CS_Results_Framework.pdf
2. Blank, M., Harkavy, I., Quinn, J., Villarreal, L., & Goodman, D. (2023). *The community schools revolution.* Retrieved from https://www.communityschoolsrevolution.org. See specifically: Martinez, L., & Hayes, C. D. (2013). *Measuring social return on investment for community schools: A case study.* Children's Aid Society; Bloodworth, M. R. & Horner, A. C. (2019). *Return on investment of a community school coordinator: A case study.* Retrieved from https://apexeval.org/wp-content/uploads/2022/06/ROI_Coordinator_ABC_2_Column_9.9.19.pdf; Economic Modeling Specialists Inc. (2012). *The economic impact of communities in schools.* Communities in Schools.
3. Bloodworth, M. R., & Horner, A. C. (2019). *Return on investment of a community school coordinator: A case study.* Retrieved from https://www.communityschools.org/wp-content/uploads/sites/2/2020/11/ROI_Coordinator.pdf
4. Illustrating the promise of community schools. Rand Corporation. Retrieved from https://www.rand.org/pubs/research_reports/RR3245.html
5. Oakes, J., Maier, A., & Daniel, J. (2017). *Community schools: An evidence-based strategy for equitable school improvement.* Boulder, CO: National Education Policy Center.

6. The Center for Popular Democracy. (2016). *Community schools: Transforming struggling schools into thriving schools.* Retrieved from https://www.populardemocracy.org/sites/default/files/Community-Schools-Layout_e.pdf
7. Patterson, T. (2022). *Community schools: Effectiveness of addressing barriers to education in suburban communities.* Honors Theses. Retrieved from https://scholar.utc.edu/honors-theses/368; Communities in Schools. (n.d.). *Our impact.* Retrieved from https://www.cistn.org/impact
8. Camera, L. (2001). *'Community schools' see revival in time of heightened need.* U.S. News & World Report. Retrieved from https://www.usnews.com/news/education-news/articles/2021-08-25/community-schools-see-revival-in-time-of-heightened-need
9. Deich, S. & Neary, M. (2020). *Financing community schools: A Framework for Growth and Sustainability.* Retrieved from https://futureforlearning.org/2020/04/16/financing-community-schools/
10. The CSLX website has excellent resources on the community school coordinator, along with other elements of community schools. CSLX. (2023). *The basics: Community School Coordinator.* Retrieved from https://cslx.org/resources/the-basics-community-school-coordinator
11. CSLX. (2023). *The basics: Community School Coordinator.* Retrieved from https://cslx.org/resources/the-basics-community-school-coordinator
12. U.S. Department of Education. (2021). *Nita M. Lowey 21st Century Community Learning Centers funding status.* Washington, DC. https://www2.ed.gov/print/programs/21stcclc/funding/html; Quinn, J. (2022). *Transforming afterschool programs into "Engines of Development": A policy analysis of the Federal 21st Century Community Learning Centers* (Doctoral dissertation, City University of New York).
13. Community Schools. (n.d.). *On boarding, site mapping, & capacity building.* Retrieved from https://sites.google.com/sandi.net/sdusd-community-schools/onboarding#h.s0m6x9gqno2n
14. New York State Community Schools Network. (2024). Retrieved from https://www.nyscsn.org
15. Information for this case study came from Blank et al. (2023). *The community schools revolution.* Retrieved from https://www.communityschoolsrevolution.org/going-big-big-apple-how-

grassroots-movement-helped-launch-nation-s-largest-citywide-community and Capers, N., & Shah, S. C. (2015). The power of community schools. *Voices in Urban Education*, *40*, 27–35.

16 Blank, M., Harkavy, I., Quinn, J., Villarreal, L., & Goodman, D. (2023). *The community schools* revolution. Retrieved from https://www.communityschoolsrevolution.org/going-big-big-apple-how-grassroots-movement-helped-launch-nation-s-largest-citywide-community, p. 110.

17 NYC Community Schools. (2024). Retrieved from https://www.schools.nyc.gov/learning/programs/community-schools

18 Woods, E. L. (2022). *The path to successful community school policy adoption: A comparative analysis of district-level policy reform processes.* Routledge.

19 Woods, E. L. (2022). *The path to successful community school policy adoption: A comparative analysis of district-level policy reform processes.* Routledge, p. 113.

20 Baltimore City Public Schools. (2014). *Community schools.* Retrieved from https://www.baltimorecityschools.org/page/community-schools.s

7

Making It Work: A Question of Equity

Introduction

While the word equity has become controversial in today's highly charged political climate, the concept of equity is at the heart of our aspirations for our students. Community schools hold promise in delivering *all* students a better path to engagement, wellness, and achievement. Regardless of whether you call community schools an equity-related initiative, it is undeniable that they shift the paradigm of "the way we do school."[1] Community school strategies and tenets make a difference in the lives of students and communities.

Let's explore the role of community schools in promoting educational equity by revisiting the first question asked in Chapter 1, "Why This, Why Now?" A compelling answer is one that is short and simple: community schools are an equity strategy, and a powerful one at that.

Several national studies highlight the connection between community schools and equity. The Equity and Excellence Commission, appointed by Congress in 2013, recommended strategies to support students in high poverty communities. These strategies, many of which are cited in this book, include a community needs assessment process, carefully cultivated

DOI: 10.4324/9781032717692-7

partnerships, increased family engagement, learning time that occurs beyond the traditional school day, and the provision of healthcare. The Commission also celebrated the work of the Cincinnati Community Learning Centers, which continues to receive accolades for their district-wide community schools initiative.[2]

The 2017 Learning Policy Institute and National Education Policy Center study (also mentioned in Chapters 1 and 6) has a section titled "Community Schools as a Response to Poverty and Inequity," in which researchers note the following:

> Community schools cannot overcome all problems facing poor neighborhoods ... they have a long history of connecting children and family to resources, opportunities, and supports that foster healthy development and help offset the harms of poverty. A health clinic can deliver medical and psychological treatment, as well as glasses to myopic children, dental care to those who need it, and inhalers for asthma suffers. Extending the school day and remaining open during the summer enables the school to offer additional academic help and activities, such as sports and music, which can entice youngsters who might otherwise drop out. Community schools can engage parents as learners as well as partners, offering them the opportunity to develop a skill, such as learning English or cooking, or preparing for a GED or citizenship exam, and it can support their efforts to improve the neighborhood—for example, by securing a stop sign or getting rid of hazardous waste.[3]

While these two national studies provide helpful descriptions of the intersection between community schools and equity, what else does it look like when community schools are a true equity strategy? How can school leaders ensure that schools continue to center equity as they progress through their community school journey?

To answer those questions, recall one of the definitions of community schools offered in Chapter 2:

Community schools are a strategy, not a program, that views both academic and out-of-school factors as key to student achievement and growth. They organize the resources and the voices of the school and community around student success, serving as a hub for the community, and they generate a sense of collective investment from the community surrounding the school.[4]

This definition of community schools evolved from community schools "of old," which were predominantly deficit-based and focused on filling gaps and providing missing services. While the new wave of community schools also provides integrated services, opportunities, and supports, they aim for so much more. These schools focus on collective impact strategies, whole school transformation, and authentic community engagement.

Over the course of my interviews, several principals used the term "equity" or "equity strategy" to describe the work at their school. However, equity is a broad term that means different things to different people, both in theory and in practice. For the purposes of discussion, let's ensure that we have a clear and shared definition.

The field of social justice education offers a framework with particular attention to underserved groups in schools.[5] Social justice researchers offer three different components of equity[6]:

Distributive: Focusing on ensuring that resources—financial, human, and programmatic—are allocated equitably and that students get what they need to achieve at the highest levels possible (leveling the proverbial resource "playing field").

Cultural: Ensuring that diverse perspectives are represented, for example, ensuring a culturally or community relevant curriculum.

Associative: Involving underserved groups, often those who have the least amount of voice and influence, in authentic decision-making processes.

Social justice researchers[7] have determined that equity-minded leaders pay attention to how each of these three social justice components manifest in their communities; they then focus on the difficult work of trying to make a difference in these areas and addressing situations in which these elements might conflict. Importantly, social justice researchers recognize that while school leaders will set the tone and must "walk the talk," they cannot advance equity alone.[8] By now, systems thinking should sound like a familiar refrain, and it applies here: equity work requires engagement by all stakeholders in the school and surrounding communities. Principals must understand and embody equity-minded thinking, and all stakeholders must share the vision.

Let's continue to explore equity through the lens of the distributive, cultural, and associative elements as seen through a community school's assets.

An Assets-Based Framework

Going back to one of the themes of community schools, we remember the need to operate from an asset-based lens, rather than a deficit mindset. As emphasized throughout this book, a deficit model focuses on what is wrong, missing, or broken. In contrast, an asset-based lens, framework, or model (I will use these terms interchangeably) focuses on strengths, ranging from skills and expertise, knowledge of the surrounding community, and knowledge of the cultures and languages the school represents. Once identified, such assets become resources for addressing community needs and priorities.

Here, as throughout this book, principals explain it best. Natoya Coleman (principal at Doyle Ryder Elementary, Flint, MI) speaks to the connection between equity and an assets-based framework.

> Equity work for me is about humanizing the person that you're serving and not looking at it from a deficit perspective or a data point. This work is about serving

human beings who come to this school with great value. I'm always hearing that these families don't have ... or these families would never have ... or these families are struggling with ... It's crucial NOT to see my families in that way. I always let my families know that I am aware that you love your child more than I ever could. And anything that I'm doing is only just adding to the love that you already have, the value that you already have, the character and culture that already exists within your home and within this community. And I think that's where we should start. The approach in which we go about doing things cannot stem from a deficit space—it needs to be a strengths-based approach.

Whether you call it a strength-based approach, as Principal Coleman did, or an assets-based approach, central to community schools is the assumption that students, families, and communities bring great value. Inherent to an assets-based approach is the belief that the community itself knows best what they need—and can play a key role in getting there. Here is where the cultural and associative elements of the framework overlap with the distributive. As Terrence Green, a leader in the field of equity in education, highlights, the principal should not think of themselves as the savior, but rather as one who advocates *"for* and *with* communities."[9] Principals "form lasting partnerships and have authentic collaboration with their surrounding communities—not just coffee with the principal."[10] And despite many challenges that exist in their communities, principals realize how their schools can be a driver in recognizing community assets and involving community members in real decision-making processes that will impact students and families.

How do principals know if they are seeing their communities through an asset-based lens? Principal Coleman offered the following:

> One would really need to do an assessment of their own position within the community and determine whether their work is filtering through a lens of bias. Oftentimes

we mean well, but the work becomes very transactional, and there is an over-emphasis on providing services to those with the greatest need. For us to get through to the transformational piece, we need to set our biases aside and think deeply about how we can build bridges and build relationships in ways that truly create transformational experiences, for not just the children, but for families as well. Sometimes we come into these situations with preconceived notions about our families, and not necessarily the will and commitment to empower them from where they are.

To explore this idea of assessing their relationship with equitable practices, I explicitly asked principals to share some questions they often ask of themselves when "checking" for biases and determining whether they are maintaining an asset-based approach.[11]

Checking for Bias—What Questions Should We Be Asking Ourselves?

1. Why am I doing community schools work in the first place?
2. What values am I embodying? What am I modeling to my staff? Am I modeling a savior mentality or am I modeling the ability to ask for help and show vulnerability?
3. Who can I partner with to help me accomplish this work? Are there times that I can step aside and let others lead?
4. Are we taking care of our most vulnerable students?
5. Am I making my school an open and welcoming place?
6. Am I, and are we, "truly listening to the perspectives of families, parents, communities, staff, and teachers"?[12] Are we creating opportunities for dialogue but not actually incorporating feedback into our practice?
7. Am I proactively seeking out relationships with parents and community members for reasons other than to move the needle on quantitative measures?

8. How are the school's interventions impacting students and families? If we cannot answer this question, or the answer is not favorable, are we changing our approach?
9. What happens when we face adversity or when others push back against our vision? In the words of Terrence Green, "Are we prepared to advocate for and sustain relentless actions toward equitable practices?"[13]

Along with carving out some time to reflect, it is important to consider the role of data in achieving educational equity. As Chuanika Sanders-Thomas, former principal of James Logan Elementary, Philadelphia, PA, shared: "When we make assumptions without grounding them in quantitative or qualitative data, we go off course."

Data and Equity

As we discussed in Chapter 5, data can serve as a hammer or a flashlight. In other words, it can be used not just to identify problems but to shine a light on possible solutions. What are some ways that principals ensure that data is, in fact, a flashlight that helps the school reveal inequities and create more equitable practices?

Former Principal Sanders explains how her fidelity to data kept her centered on impact:

> As a principal, I was always focused on understanding what the data was telling me. I would review a program over three to six months and ask, "How has it impacted our students?" It always came back to the question of impact. If you can't quantify the impact, if you can't say students are coming to school more joyful or engaged, or that something positive is happening with students or families, then it's likely not an equitable practice.

She then added that the work required to create and maintain a community school must emanate from the people it is serving, especially from the data surfaced through the needs and assets assessment.

> In a community school, we use needs assessments, conversations, and focus groups with families, students, and the community to ensure we're providing what people want while aligning our practices with rigorous academic expectations. It's about meeting people where they are while also building on their existing skills to help them access better schools or career opportunities. When parents don't approve of or understand a partnership in the school, that signals a problem. It could mean the partnership hasn't been communicated effectively or is not meeting the community's needs. In either case, it suggests that the partnership may not be the equitable practice we need.

Programming and partnerships are only two areas in which equity must be examined through a data lens. Other areas include teacher quality and achievement. For example, principals can compare teachers with the highest combination of qualifications and experience against students with the highest needs. Are the students with the highest needs getting access to these teachers, or are they working with less qualified teachers? Data can also be used to uncover inequalities in areas such as the representation of certain subgroups of students in special education. In addition to the traditional achievement data, principals can analyze standardized testing scores and representation of students in different tracks (e.g. college prep) from an equity perspective.[14] As researcher James Coviello explains, the concept of data-driven decision-making becomes more powerful when principals use these types of skills to better understand elements of equity.[15]

Whether it is guiding their school's approach to data or modeling behavior for the staff, students, and community, the principal is the steward of the equity minded mission. The principal cannot alone create an equity-minded school, but the school will not achieve equity without a principal who embodies and leads with an equity mindset.

To embrace the community school strategy, leaders must imagine education differently. To some degree, there must be a mindset shift. School leaders and leadership teams must start with an equity mindset and hold the belief that traditionally under-resourced and vulnerable students and their families deserve the same access and opportunities afforded to students in more affluent communities. This includes voice and agency in prioritizing needs, designing solutions, and confronting the inherent complexities and oftentimes frustrating limitations of the role of principal.

Closing Thoughts

To close out this book, let's review what has been covered. The earliest chapters in this book explored the need for community schools and subsequent call for action, posing the questions "Why community schools, and why now?" These chapters highlight some of the differences between community schools and more traditional schools and define key terms used in the community schools movement.

Chapter 3 articulates the development of vision statements to align members of the school community around a common set of goals. The chapter also covers building of trust with school staff, creating collaborative leadership structures, and developing "mini principals" throughout the school. Chapter 4 turns to elevating and investing in the role of the community school coordinator, being an effective coach, and partnering throughout the needs and assets assessment process. This chapter also highlights the difference between involvement and engagement by parents and the larger community.

Chapters 5 and 6 focus on data and advocacy. Chapter 5 introduces the metaphor of data as a flashlight, rather than a hammer, reinforcing that gathering, interpreting, and effectively utilizing data is the responsibility of all constituents. This chapter also explains the use of logic models to help identify what data needs to be collected to achieve desired results, build a shared community understanding of what the community school is trying to achieve, and help generate actions that will improve practice. Chapter 6 then pivots to advocacy, making a case for increased funding, and creating the "urgency" in which the intended audience cannot say no. Chapter 6 also shares strategies to ground advocacy in the context of national data and use elevator pitches to advocate for sustainable community schools. It also presents case studies of districts in which community school advocates rallied together to change city and district policy.

And in this final chapter, we have just explored how community schools, by their very nature, assist with creating educational equity.

Whether from this book, a technical assistance resource online, or a mentor principal in another district, I hope you will take the opportunity to learn as much as you can: the possibilities of leading a community school are limitless. Earlier, I noted that community schools have evolved over time. As some of the most significant players in this field, principals, both established or emerging, will continue to define the community school movement. I invite you to join in shaping the growth and evolution of your school in ways that honor the richness and uniqueness of your own community.

Final Question for Principals: What Would You Tell Your Past or Future Self?

I wish I had spent more time thinking about how to share some of what we were able to create at our community school with others. I wish I had spent more time getting the information out there.

(Amy Randolph, former Principal of Oyler School, Pre k-12, Cincinnati Ohio, and current Assistant Superintendent, Cincinnati Public Schools

Here is the advice I would give my past self. Approach each meeting and each person you encounter as if you just got hired and are learning about the job. Push yourself to engage with people and not just "administrivia." Also, I would tell myself to resist the temptation to become stagnant. Figure out anew each day, each year, each community school coordinator, what we are in that moment, while never losing the ideas and learnings that we had in the past. Always pay attention to what is working. And always continue to learn and push your practice.

(Mark Gaither, Principal of Wolfe Street Academy Baltimore, Maryland)

The journey ahead is going to be the toughest thing you have ever done, but it is also going to be the most rewarding and impactful. You are going to see positive, tremendous growth in your school, school community, and the systems that support them, but the greatest growth will be in yourself. Your best self will emerge through this work. The relationships you establish will be some of the most deep and loyal you will ever develop. It's okay to say it is hard, to get tired, or even occasionally discouraged at the mountain ahead. But after taking just a few seconds, look at that mountain and realize that within a few short years, it will be only a fraction of the size it is now, and it will have a clear pathway of success carved through it that others can use to find their way forward. So keep going and do not ever shy away from the hard work. You were brought to this moment for this reason. Enjoy the ride! You are so much stronger on the other side.

(Bethany Groves, Principal at Webster Elementary, St. Augustine, Florida)

Notes

1. Fernández, A. (2020). *BPS Hub Schools Town Hall.* National Center for Community Schools. (2024). *Every school a community school.* Retrieved from https://www.nccs.org
2. Kotting, J. (2022). *Greater Cincinnati's community learning centers lead place-based learning and holistic neighborhood development.* Brookings. Retrieved from https://www.brookings.edu/articles/greater-cincinnatis-community-learning-centers-lead-place-based-learning-and-holistic-neighborhood-development/

3   Illustrating the promise of community schools. Rand Corporation. Retrieved from https://www.rand.org/pubs/research_reports/RR3245.html. See also Quinn, J., & Blank, M. J. (2020). Twenty years, ten lessons: Community schools as an equitable school improvement strategy. *VUE (Voices in Urban Education)*, *49*(2), 44–53; Rogers, J. S. (1998). *Community schools: Lessons from the past and present*. Los Angeles, CA: University of California, Los Angeles's Institute for Democracy, Education, and Access.

4   This definition is loosely adapted from a presentation given by Abe Fernández (Director of the National Center for Community Schools) and the following document: IEL (2014). *Community schools are an essential equity strategy*. Retrieved from https://www.communityschools.org/wp-content/uploads/sites/2/2021/01/CS-Equity-Framework-Final-Working-Draft.pdf

5   DeMatthews, D., & Mawhinney, H. (2014). Social justice leadership and inclusion: Exploring challenges in an urban district struggling to address inequities. *Educational Administration Quarterly*, *50*(5), 844–881.

6   Gewirtz, S., & Cribb, A. (2002). Plural conceptions of social justice: Implications for policy sociology. *Journal of Education Policy*, *17*(5), 499–509.

7   Coviello, J. (2017). What every principal should know about social justice leadership. *Instructional Leader*, *30*(6), 9–12.

8   Coviello, J. (2017). What every principal should know about social justice leadership. *Instructional Leader*, *30*(6), 9–12, p. 10.

9   Green, T. L. (2017). Community-based equity audits: A practical approach for educational leaders to support equitable community-school improvements. *Educational Administration Quarterly*, *53*(1), 3–39, p. 6.

10 Coviello, J. (2017). What every principal should know about social justice leadership. *Instructional Leader*, *30*(6), 9–12, p. 10.

11 Questions 6 and 9 did not come directly from principals, rather from Terrance Green's thoughtful and comprehensive work on Equity Audits. Green, T. L. (2023). *Equity audits that make real change*. Retrieved from website: terrance@raciallyjustschools.com, p. 12.

12 Green, T. L. (2023). *Equity audits that make real change*. Retrieved from website: terrance@raciallyjustschools.com, p. 12.

13 Green, T. L. (2023). *Equity audits that make real change*. Retrieved from website: terrance@raciallyjustschools.com, p. 15.
14 Skrla, L., Scheurich, J. J., Garcia, J., & Nolly, G. (2004). Equity audits: A practical leadership tool for developing equitable and excellent schools. *Educational Administration Quarterly*, *40*(1), 133–161.
15 Coviello, J. (2017). What every principal should know about social justice leadership. *Instructional Leader*, *30*(6), 9–12.

Appendix A

(Introduction, p. 8)

Stages of Development

	Emerging	Maturing	Transforming
Characteristics / what you would see in a CS at this stage	• Champions for community school call for the strategy and have developed an implementation team • School community members are oriented to the strategy • Setting priorities for implementation identified • Desire to use data collaboratively for whole school transformation • Data is shared with champions; new data interests and needs are identified • Common understanding of community assets and needs (A&N) • New systems and approaches to schooling are emerging (i.e. whole school approach to restorative practices)	• New youth, family, and community members are identified as leaders in the school and structures to promote community voice, reflection, and partnerships are developed • Shared governance is visible • Shared vision and goals are set for the CS based on A&N • Data analysis begins and committees try practices such as "plan, do, study, act" • New systems and approaches to schooling are codified in this phase • Moving from outputs to outcomes • Gaps have been identified and resources are connected to opportunities • Community school has many feedback loops • Alignment between budget and CS priorities	• Community leadership structures formalized, co-led, and co-created; all community members, families, youth, and partners involved in processes • Policies support CS sustainability & community voice • All structures engage in continuous improvement • Community school guides other schools and systems to enact CS strategy • Affinity groups for youth and staff support equity work • Plans exist for transition and orientation of new community members
Processes/Structures/ Tasks / what CS constituents would do at this stage	**Develop or start with an existing group of families, youth, teachers, administrators, and community partners to enact the following implementation functions:** • Conduct an assets and needs assessment • Utilize power analysis to determine which constituents to engage as champions • School based data review • Orient all school community members to the strategy • Community asset mapping to identify potential partners **Additional tasks during this phase:** • Hire a Community School Coordinator • Develop or utilize an existing ISS team using data (such as chronic absence) to begin connecting students to supports • Develop youth and family leadership structures	**Group responsible for Implementation will:** • Support co-constructed initiatives based on Assets & Needs assessment • Formalize partnerships with a written agreement, such as a MOU or shared use agreement for space and data sharing and management. • Develop clear CS vision and goals and share with larger community **Additional tasks during this phase:** • Structures in place to align classroom instruction with community & extended opportunities • Build/identify designated room specifically for families/guardians • CSC and other CS staff members are sustained through diverse funding sources	**Group responsible for Implementation will:** • Lead participatory budgeting process or practice budget transparency • Codify policies for sustainability with equity focus • Coordinate advocacy efforts **Additional tasks during this phase:** • Family and youth advocate for policy and address systemic inequities • Youth and community led initiatives, such as: conferences/town halls, YPAR projects occur annually • Piloted initiatives evolve into new "way of doing school" • All community members involved in community school continuous improvement
Measures/ Benchmarks / what to measure at each stage	• Chronic absence • Program attendance • Enrollment • Discipline • Service use • Student & family engagement • Youth feedback/voice (ie. Hope Survey)	• School climate surveys • Student and staff retention • Staff turnover • Academic growth • Return on investment (ROI)	• Graduation rates • Post-secondary enrollment • Deeper learning & deep listening • Workforce development • Economic development • Micro credentials & Certificates for teachers/staff/partners

Appendix B

Path to a Vision: Oyler School, Cincinnati Ohio (Pre K-12)

At Oyler[1], the vision development process took place over one summer. The first step was a staff retreat for the instructional leadership team, made up of team leads from each grade and department. At the retreat, each team member shared their perspective on the key values they believed should be central to the vision and remain consistent even across wide age range that the school covered.

The next step was a series of surveys and discussions with our teachers, followed by a two-day off-site retreat off site with teacher leaders, the resource coordinator [community school coordinator], the family engagement specialist, and two partners.

After this retreat, the team sat down, compiled all the feedback from the staff and partners, and drafted a statement. The statement was first presented to the entire staff for feedback, then reviewed by the local School Decision-Making Committee, which included community partners, community members, parents, teachers, and administrators. It's important to mention that the students weren't involved as much as they could have since the process took place during the summer. However, as (former) principal Amy Randolph explained, "many different stakeholders were able to give their unique perspectives, leading us to the vision statement we have now."

Oyler Mission and Vision Statements

Mission Statement

Oyler Community Learning Center, in partnership with families, community members, and local agencies, will foster academic excellence, cultivate student confidence, and create leadership opportunities. Oyler strives to produce graduates who will persevere through life and become responsible and productive members of society.

Vision Statement

All students who enter Oyler Community Learning Center will graduate on time, prepared to achieve their post-secondary goals.

Community Learning Center

We are very proud to be a Community Learning Center and a neighborhood anchor. We strive to go beyond academics to focus on the whole child. We do this by serving as a hub for services that are available to students, their families, and the entire community. We are able to offer a variety of services thanks to the support of our many partners and the Oyler community.

Note

1 Please note that in Ohio, they use the term "Community Learning Centers" not community schools; the term Community School often refers to charter schools.

Appendix C

Assets and Needs Assessment Toolkit

Why an Assets and Needs Assessment? Test
An assets and needs assessment is a systematic process used to understand and create a profile of a community school's needs. Without a current and comprehensive assets and needs assessment, a community school is less likely to provide offerings or foster partnerships that effectively address risks and promote opportunities for all of its students and families. The purpose of the assets and assets and needs assessment is NOT to rigorously or scientifically evaluate the impact of individual programs, strategies, and curricula, but instead to gather a wide range of information that will inform and drive decisions about the community school's programming and operations.

How was the Assets and Needs Assessment Toolkit developed?
This Toolkit was developed by Children's Aid National Center for Community Schools in partnership with the leadership and staff of the Chicago Public Schools Community School Initiative (CSI), an advisory group composed of representatives from key CSI Lead Agencies and the New York-based research firm ActKnowledge. The toolkit builds on the collective strengths and experiences of all of the aforementioned and includes adaptations of the Plus 50 Needs Assessment Toolkit developed by the American Association of Community Colleges.

What's included in the Toolkit?
The Toolkit was designed to be user-friendly and as brief as possible. It is organized around the key steps of the assets and needs assessment process, which are listed below and best completed in sequence:

1. Getting Started
2. Archival Data Review
3. Initial Analysis
4. Surveys
5. Key Stakeholder Interviews
6. Focus Groups
7. Final Analysis
8. Reporting

Depending on your community school's practice, you may already have some of the above steps in place, in which case it is entirely appropriate to include those existing resources into this process. Each step is described in the same format. You will see the following under each:

Tasks: Key activities or strategies that should be taken
Tips: Best practice suggestions to consider and pitfalls to avoid
Tools: Worksheets or sample instruments that can be used to support the process

The Assets and Needs Assessment Toolkit is available digitally and can be easily adapted to meet your particular needs.

Assets & Needs Assessment Stages
Step 1: Getting Started

Tasks	• Convene the Advisory Council • Revisit the Advisory Council's mission/purpose and consider whether to add members • Conduct a Readiness Self-Assessment
Tips	• You should not need to create a new team to take on the data gathering and analysis responsibilities. Conducting assets and needs assessments should be one of the core functions of the community school's Advisory Council. The process described in this Toolkit may serve as an opportunity to reengage key stakeholders in your school and neighborhood and activate your Advisory Council. • Consider the existing diversity of experience, skills and perspectives of the Advisory Council to help you identify which potential new members you need. • One person should act as the project manager to keep track of the overall process and keep team members accountable.
Tools	*Buiding Your Team Worksheet* *Readiness Self-Assessment Worksheet*

Step 2: Archival Data Review

Tasks	• Gather and record key information from existing data sources (such as attendance—both average daily and chronic absenteeism; grades; school suspension rates/behavior incidents; after-school attendance; community health statistics; median income; crime rates, demographics; culture and climate ratings; etc.) • Manipulate existing data sources to deepen your understanding (determining the chronic absence rates of English Language Learners, for example, will require some reworking of existing data sets) • Complete the Archival Data Collection Worksheet
Tips	• Make full use of the data reports provided by local and state education agencies and other public and private sources (US Census data, collective impact initiatives, community action associations, foundations, etc.) • As you collect and record each datum, new questions will likely come to mind, as might concerns about the accuracy of the data. Record those questions, concerns, and other thoughts on the Worksheet. • Add Need Indicators to the worksheet as needed and appropriate. Blank rows have been inserted for this purpose.
Tools	*Archival Data Collection Worksheet and Resource Inventory Worksheet*

Step 3: Initial Analysis

| Tasks | - Convene Advisory Council to review the Archival Data
- Identify the top five high-priority needs that emerge from the review
- Brainstorm particular questions that should be considered for the survey, interview, and focus group steps
- Identify the key stakeholders to be interviewed in Step 5 |
|---|---|
| Tips | - Remember that this is an *initial* analysis and that you are not expected to have findings at this point.
- The purpose, instead, is to collectively identify patterns and see connections between the need indicators and begin to narrow the focus of your needs assessment. |
| Tools | *Archival Data Collection Worksheet*
Resource Inventory Worksheet |

Step 4: Gather Voices - Surveys

| Tasks | - Develop surveys for key constituent groups. Surveys of students, parents, and teachers are required, but others may be added.
- Administer the surveys
- Compile survey results |
|---|---|
| Tips | - Questions should be mostly closed-ended (multiple choice, true/false, Likert Scales, etc.) and limited in number.
- Paper vs. Online (using the method or combination of methods most likely to ensure a high response rate)
- Use vocabulary and language that is appropriate for each audience. In all cases, avoid using technical language and terminology.
- Particularly for youth surveys, you might consider offerings incentives.
- Decide whether to use a paper-based or web-based survey (or both). Each has its advantages and disadvantages, but web-based surveys are especially convenient because they can tally up and graphically present responses automatically. There are free and low cost solutions out there. When using paper, it may make sense to record the responses on an electronic spreadsheet.
- Timing the administration of surveys to coincide with, for example, faculty meetings, parent-teacher conferences, after-school special events may increase the yield of responses. |
| Tools | *Gathering Voices: Surveys*
Sample Survey |

Step 5: Gather Voices — Key Stakeholder Interviews

Tasks	• Conduct Key Stakeholder Interviews • Summarize findings
Tips	• Keep interviews to 30–45 minutes long • Decide whether you want the same person conducting all of the interviews for the sake of consistency. • Do your best to frame questions in a way that elicits the key stakeholders' interpretation of the data and perhaps some suggestions for addressing the needs • Avoid making the stakeholder feel defensive; keep the conversation focused on the ways in which students may require supports and opportunities, and away from what they themselves have or have not done to address those needs
Tools	*Key Stakeholder Interview Worksheet* *Sample Interview Questions*

Step 6: Gather Voices — Focus Groups

Tasks	• Conduct Focus Groups. Groups including students, parents, and teachers are required, but others may be added. • Summarize findings
Tips	• Focus groups are generally most lively and effective when composed of 6–12 people They should last between 45 and 60 minutes. Consider your audience when scheduling the focus groups (i.e. evenings or weekends for working parents, in-school hours for teachers if possible) • You will need a facilitator and a note taker. Do not combine these roles if possible as it is exceedingly difficult to do both simultaneously. • Prepare a scripted introduction and 8–12 questions in advance (samples are provided for you). Unlike with the surveys, questions in focus groups should be open-ended and should encourage participants to elaborate. • Ask participants to follow up on and react to each other's responses • Stay away from yes/no questions.
Tools	*Sample Focus Group Scripts and Questions*

Appendix C: Assets and Needs Assessment Tool ◆ 163

Step 7: Final Analysis

Tasks	• Convene Advisory Council to review summaries of surveys, interviews, and focus groups • Determine three priority need areas for the next 12 months • Review and brainstorm additional recommendations for how to address the needs
Tips	• Advisory Council members should receive—in advance of the final analysis convening—summaries of the survey, interview, and focus group results. • Schedule enough time to have a thorough reflection and discussion. • If needed, schedule a second session to ensure completion.
Tools	*Assets and Needs Assessment Analysis Worksheet*

Step 8: Reporting

Tasks	• Write Assets and Need Assessment Report • Disseminate Report
Tips	• Resist the urge to over think, over format or over produce this report. Bulleted lists are more readable—and therefore more actionable—than narrative descriptions. • Include completed worksheets from the toolkit as supporting material in an appendix. • The report itself should focus on your identified findings, priorities, and recommendations.
Tools	*Assets and Needs Assessment Analysis Worksheet (completed, from Step 7)* *Assets and Needs Assessment Report Outline*

Appendix D

Community Schools Communications Toolkit[1]

The Coalition for Community Schools, an initiative of the Institute for Educational Leadership, has developed this communications toolkit as the go-to resource for materials for effectively communicating the transformative impact of Community Schools. As advocates for comprehensive and community-driven education, the Coalition understands the importance of clear, compelling messaging. This information can guide organizers and supporters of the Community Schools movement in outreach to communities and lawmakers.

Bi-Partisan Messaging: Communicating about the Value of Community Schools

These key messages can be utilized in communicating about the benefits of embracing and advancing the Community School strategy and are meant to help garner bipartisan support at the local, state, and national levels.

Guidance on the differentiated messaging:

- ♦ Underlined messages have been developed with progressive or left leaning audiences in mind.
- ♦ *Italicized* messages have been developed with more conservative audiences in mind.
  - The term "Community Schools" can be used or replaced with terminology more appropriate for your region.

---

[1] Coalition for Community Schools, an initiative of IEL. (n.d.). Community schools communications toolkit. Retrieved from https://docs.google.com/document/d/16qzcPcY882dRpXT2t3E0gUVjvWTK8OmC4jOaeCaw_k8/edit?tab=t.0

Key Talking Point: Introducing and Defining Community Schools

Community Schools provide students and their communities with innovative learning environments and support systems that young people need to thrive in school, college, and the workplace.

Community Schools unite schools and families around access to quality education that prepares students for success in the workplace and in our communities.

- Community Schools are public schools that combine resources and people throughout a community to expand learning opportunities and support for all students.
- Community Schools provide a local engagement strategy for creating and coordinating opportunities with public schools to accelerate student, family, and community success.
- Community Schools are learning hubs that unite families, educators, and community partners around a strategy to promote equity-centered practices that improve long-term life changes of today's students.
- *Community Schools are growing in popularity because research shows they can improve student outcomes, while also being cost-efficient and locally controlled.*
- Schools and communities are stronger together.

Key Talking Point: Community Schools Have Momentum

Schools and communities are uniting to transform learning and bring greater opportunity and equity to school systems across America.

Communities and schools are teaming up to create learning environments that focus on improving efficiencies of academic and non-academic resources, to accelerate student outcomes.

- In a Community School, parents play an active role in their children's education.
- Student needs have grown beyond what traditional schools alone can meet.

- Communities have untapped resources that can help schools meet the learning needs of all students and give them the skills and inspiration to thrive.
- Today, there are more than (##) Community Schools in (##) states across the nation providing new support and options for children in cities, suburbs, and rural areas.
- Community Schools can go by different names, but they share a common theme of uniting communities to accelerate student success.
- *Community Schools focus on making sure each student is healthy, safe, engaged, supported, and challenged.*
- <u>Schools need all the resources available in a community to provide fair and equitable learning options and ensure children's needs are adequately met in and out of school.</u>
- Community Schools provide locally determined resources and support for students outside of the classroom —such as counseling services, nutrition programs, and targeted instructional strategies—so students can thrive in the classroom.
- Political differences fade when communities become equal partners in student learning.

Key Talking Point: Community Schools Improve Outcomes and Opportunity

<u>Community Schools are an effective and proven strategy for improving education while using culturally informed strategies that help all students reach their potential academically and in the future.</u>

Community Schools are an improvement strategy incorporating all factors that impact learning for better student outcomes.

- Community Schools support the whole child so that they are ready to focus and learn when they are in school.
- *Communities that unite with their schools can expect higher attendance, greater family engagement, better conditions for learning, and improved confidence in schools.*

- <u>A community school strategy makes it easier to focus teaching and learning to connect classroom curriculum to real-world community issues, student interests, and learning opportunities.</u>
- Academic success is accelerated when community resources focus on student health, tutoring, after-school and summer enrichment, mentorships, and other supports.
- There are many examples of Community Schools producing impressive gains for students and their communities:
  - After five years of using a Community Schools strategy, Webb Middle School in Austin, Texas, became the city's highest performing middle school.
  - One Orlando, Florida, high school increased enrollment by more than 500 students while cutting disciplinary incidents in half and more than doubling industry certifications.
  - After eight years as a Community School, an elementary school in Baltimore, Maryland, ranked second in the city academically and reading proficiency reached 95% for fifth graders.

Key Talking Point: Community Schools Are Cost-Effective

<u>Community Schools are cost-effective stewards of public and private funds, maximizing student support and delivery of services to meet student and community needs.</u>

Community Schools are cost-effective, efficient, and promise returns on our investments for schools, students, and our communities.

- Community Schools bring funding and resources into schools that would otherwise not be available.
- Community Schools can increase funds and other resources for students by catalyzing public investment and combining funding and resources.
- Community Schools secure mixed short- and long-term funding from multiple sources to develop a sustainable funding base.

♦ Diverse funding and resources come from public and private sources to support both infrastructure and key services as well as costs for starting up and adding programs.
  • One case study shows that each $1 invested in a Community Schools Coordinator returns over $7 in net benefits to a community.

Key Talking Point: Community Schools Effectively Engage Families and Communities

<u>Community Schools authentically engage families, community organizations, and others to advance student learning and outcomes.</u>

Community Schools foster environments where parents and caregivers become equal partners in guiding their child's education.

♦ Parents and communities have more input into the operation, direction, and outcomes of Community Schools.
♦ Community Schools are positioned to serve as a vehicle for hyper-local decision-making that responds to the unique needs of each community.
♦ Learning can happen anywhere and at any time in communities that partner with schools.
♦ <u>Local educators, partners, families, and community members collaborate to guide learning through a shared understanding of local needs and assets.</u>
♦ Communities work together in innovative ways to find and use new and existing resources to support learning and address local issues in a local context.
♦ *Community Schools create space for hyper-local decision-making between parents, communities, and educators to make it easier to meet the needs of each learner.*

The following table shows specific asks, considerations, and messages to utilize when building out your materials and talking points for meetings with policy makers, educational leaders, and district officials.

Appendix D: Community Schools Communications Toolkit ◆ 169

Audience: Policy Makers/Ed Leaders/District Officials

Amplification Message Map: Communicating with Community School Audiences

Key Ask 1: Support funding for Community Schools	*Key Ask 2: Support legislation that brings Community Schools to more districts*	*Key Ask 3: Encourage your colleagues to support community school legislation*
Key Message 1: Community Schools are a bipartisan, effective, and efficient strategy for improving education and supporting student success.	Key Message 1: A Community Schools strategy is designed and well suited to address urgent student, family, and community needs in times of crises, as we've seen during the global Coronavirus pandemic. Community Schools offer comprehensive recovery plan in an environment where education must evolve.	Key Message 1: Districts and states want to adopt this strategy. Encouraging your peers to consider or learn about Community Schools makes them more inclined to support future legislation.
Key Message 2: Significantly increasing public funding for the Full-Service Community Schools program would enable hundreds more communities to coordinate the assets of their schools, families, and community partners for students' immediate and long-term success.	Key Message 2: Community Schools are hyper-local. A Community Schools strategy puts more power in the hands of parents and families. Significantly increasing public funding for the Full-Service Community Schools program would enable hundreds more communities to coordinate the assets of their schools, families, and community partners for students' immediate and long-term success.	Key Message 2: By signaling support—you can make Community School policies topics of conversations on key committees like education and appropriations.
Key Message 3: Throughout the COVID-19 pandemic, Community Schools were able to mobilize quickly and effectively to support the social, emotional, physical, and learning needs of students and their families.	Key Message 3: Community Schools operate in a dynamic, changing environment. Through a guiding framework, technical support, and the right resources and infrastructure, local educators, partners, families, and community members engage in a deep and collaborative process to develop a comprehensive understanding of local needs and assets.	Key Message 3: Showcasing model Community Schools in your area can help set the bar/set an example for others and establish you as a leader in reimagining public education success.

Index

Note: Pages in *italics* represent figures and **bold** indicates tables in the text. Page numbers followed by "n" represent notes.

ABC Community School
    Partnership study (2019) 7, 126
advocacy 15–16, 122–128,
    151–152; and coalition
    building 132–133; community
    and coalitions (support for
    community schools) 133–135;
    creating broad advocacy team
    (case studies) 132–135
Ambrose, Stephanie 47, 65–66
assets and needs assessment
    toolkit 159–163; archival
    data review 160–161; final
    analysis 162–163; gathering
    input (surveys/interviews/
    focus groups) 161–162; initial
    analysis 161; report 163
asset-based model 29, 36, 41, 80,
    89, 146–148
asset mapping process 81
Azcoitia, Carlos 37, 88

Battaglia, Chris 70, 135
Biden, Joe 6
Blank, Marty 11
Blasio, Bill de 133
Buena Vista/Horace Mann K-8
    school, San Francisco, CA 44

California: California Community
    Schools Partnership Grant
    Program 6; investment in
    community schools in 5–6
Calvin, Sandi 1, 3

Campbell, Casey 63
Christmas Tree model 33, 74
chronic absenteeism 5, 115, 119,
    137
Cincinnati Public Schools (CPS)
    92
Coalition for Community Schools
    10, 102; Communications
    Toolkit (*see* Community
    Schools Communications
    Toolkit (Coalition for
    Community Schools))
Coalition for Educational Justice
    132
Coan, Chris 12, 79
Cohen, Jonathan 96
Coleman, Natoya 146–148
Coleman Report (1960s) 3
collaborative leadership 15, 22,
    24, 29–30, 37, 46, 49–57, 96,
    102, 151
Collaborative Partners Team
    75–76, **77–78**, 112
Communities in Schools
    organization 127
Community Learning Centers,
    Cincinnati 144, 158, 158n1
Community Partnership Schools
    138
Community School Leadership
    Team 65–67, 75–76, 81, 89–90,
    110–112, 115
Community School Policy (2016),
    Baltimore 134

community schools: champions 135–137; collection of data 76–80; common team structures at **76**; communicating with audiences 169; community resources **77–78**; data and evaluation at 95–99; definitions of 23–30, 145, 165; different models of 30; financing and sustaining (*see* financing and sustainable funding); four-pillar approach 24–25; framework for student success *98*; growth of 5–7; interconnectedness of 13, 25, 27, 35, 40, 107; key practices 25–27; leadership team 65–67, 75–76; matching needs to resources 80–81; old *vs.* new 31–33; rationale for 3–5; readiness for 40; team effort 81–83; trends over 30 years **32**
Community Schools Communications Toolkit (Coalition for Community Schools) 132, 164–168; bi-partisan messaging 164; cost-effectiveness 167–168; defining community schools 165; engagement of families and communities 168; improvement of outcomes and opportunity 166–167; learning environments 165–166
community schools coordinator (CSC) 16, 21–22, 28–30, 49, 62–67, **65**, 83, 85, 106, 118, 123, 128; full-time 128–129; high-level resource 28, 62, 64, 70; importance of maximizing 106; key characteristics 67–70; key responsibilities 65–67; and principals 64, 67, 69–72, 75, 116–117, 136; schools that don't have funding for 72–73; *vs.* CSD 64

Community Schools Forward 8, 25–26; Essentials for Community School Transformation *26*, 110, *111*
Community Schools Learning Exchange (CSLX) 64
Community Schools Playbook 27
Community Schools Revolution 108–109, 133
comprehensive community school legislation 6
conceptual skills 13, 52, 69
Consortium on Chicago School research 30
context-specific approach 22, 30–31
Cortes, Migdalia 86
COVID-19 pandemic 4–5, 119
cross-boundary leadership 10–12, 14, 58
CSLX website 141n10

data, community schools 5; for advocacy 122–128; analyzing 69, 74–76, 82, 106, 138, 150; collection of (new) data 75–80, 82, 91, 95–96, 99, 124, 138, 151; and equity 149–151; and evaluation 95–99; existing school and community data 75, 129; as a flashlight 96, 149, 151; as a hammer 96, 149, 151; informing school vision 66; logic model 99; principals on 117–119, 125; Return on Investment (ROI) 7, 19n16, 125–126, 140n2-3; using to reveal inequities 149
Dehn, Shane 68
Deich, Sharon 108
Delarios-Morán, Claudia 16–17, 43–44, 50, 85, 87, 101, 104
DeTablan, Dante 136
district-led model 30

elevator pitch 15, 55, 112, 124, 130–132, 137–140, 152
Equity and Excellence Commission 143–144
equity, educational 143–145, 152; and data 149–151; principals on equitable practices 148–149; social justice components of 145–146
Essien, Michael 36–37, 74, 96

Fairfax County Community Schools Logic Model 102, *104*
family engagement. *see* parent engagement
Federal Full Service Community Schools program 25
Federal Funding Sources for Community Schools 109
Fernández, Abe, presentation of Community Schools 32–33, 154n4
Finance Project (2012) study 7, 125
financing and sustainable funding 107–108, *108*; accessing and redeploying existing resources 108–109; finding new funding resources 112; grant-related funding 113–117; integrating and leveraging resources 109–112
Financing Community Schools: A Framework for Growth and Sustainability 109; on creating new resources 112
Financing Community Schools: Leveraging Resources to Support Student Success 109
Finnigan, Kara S. 18n8
fist to five visual gesture tool 45–46
Florida, investment in community schools 6, 118, 138
Follette, Patricia 57, 139–140

Ford Elementary School, Lynn, MA 52–53
four-pillar approach 24–25
Frieze, Debbie 51–52
Frye, Anthony 58, 118
Full-Service Community Schools 6; Grant Awards Program 99, 113, 116

Gaither, Mark 34, 54–55, 78–80, 106–107, 136–137, 153; on data 125; role in advocacy 128–129; Team of Rivals leadership team 54
Gomes, Jo 82
Gordon IV, Richard M. 118
grant writing process 113–116
Green, Terrence 147, 149
Groves, Bethany 119, 153

Hanna, Ann 1, 36, 82
Harvey, Patricia 2, 32
human leadership skills 13, 48, 53, 69

IEL Community School Logic Model *103*
Institute for Educational Leadership 72, 102, 123
instructional leadership team 10, 17, 59, 66–67
integrated partners/partnerships/system 62, 75, 83–8, 91–92
Ishimaru, Ann 89

Jaramillo, Nicole 17; teams and leadership opportunities 55–56
Johnson, Jerry 80–81

Katz, Robert 13
Kida, Luann 16
Kiger, Theresa 137–138
Kim, Queena 48–49, 104, 106
Knapp, Jo-Anne 35

Lavaland Elementary school, Albequerque, NM 55
lead agency model 30
leader-as-hero 51
leader-as-host 51–52, 54
leadership skills 13–14, 53; collaborative leadership 15, 22, 24, 29–30, 37, 46, 49–57, 96, 102, 151; cross-boundary leadership 10–12, 14, 58; human leadership skills 13, 48, 53, 69; leadership team 10 17, 59, 65–67, 75–76; lone wolf stage of leadership 58–59; shared leadership 50; teams and leadership opportunities 55–56; three-skill approach to 13–14
Learning Policy Institute (LPI) study (2017) 109, 126, 144
Lee, Bill 127
Lloyd, Ellen 89
logic model 15, 99–100, 116, 151; Fairfax County Community Schools Logic Model 102, *104*; final logic model 102; IEL Community School Logic Model *103*; inputs/activities/outputs/outcomes *100*; sample logic models 102, 104, 106–107; and school vision 100–101, *101*; Wayne County Full-Service Community Schools Logic Model *105*
lone wolf stage of leadership 58–59

Maryland, investment in community schools in 6
McSwain, Kristin 113
memorandum of understanding (MOU) 84–85
mini principals 54, 151

Nanus, Bert, *Visionary Leadership* 42
National Center for Community Schools (NCCS) 8, 72, 83, 123; *Leading with Purpose and Passion: A Guide for Community School Directors* 72
National Education Association (NEA) 82
National Education Policy Center study 126; "Community Schools as a Response to Poverty and Inequity" 144
Neary, Meghan 108
needs and assets assessment (NAA) process 6, 15, 31, 36–37, 40, 92, 96, 115, 150–151; choosing partners/partnerships 84, 123, 138; definition of 29, 73; importance of 73–75; outside school 22; role of CSC 106; school vision and results 109–110; through community school leadership team 65, 81–83; as tool for school vision 46, 62, 66
Nerich, Amy 52
No Child Left Behind 1

Oakes, Jeannie 4
out-of-school factors 4, 96, 108, 129, 131, 134
Oxfam organization 11
Oyler School, Cincinnati Ohio (Pre-K–12) 157–158

parent academies 90
parent engagement 15, 34, 87, 151; *vs.* parent involvement 88–91
Partnership Round Table *86*
principals of community school 9–10, 16–17, 45, 53, 146; and CSCs 64, 67, 69–72, 75,

116–117, 136; on data 117–119; on elevator pitch 137–140; eliminating hierarchy 71; and equitable practices 148–149; on family engagement 90; fears of being 33–35; on integrated partners 91–92; on lone wolf stage of leadership 58–59; on mini principals 54, 151; on past or future self 152–153; power mapping exercise 56; role of 11; on traditional model 35–37; on vision/vision development 42, 47–48
Provinzano, Kathleen 71–72
PW Moore Elementary School, Elizabeth City, NC 47

Quinn, Jane 29, 40, 112

Race to the Top program 1–2
RAND corporation study 7–8, 126
Randolph, Amy 92, 152, 157
Return on Investment (ROI) data 7, 19n16, 125–126, 140n2–3
Rizzo, Pio 138
Rogus, Joseph 45
Roscup, Jay 113–115

Sanchez Gregory, Veronica 71
Sanders-Thomas, Chuanika 22, 106, 149
Santiago, Eileen 58–59, 91–92
shared leadership model 50
shared vision 43, 50
social justice education 145–146
Stages of Development Tool, NCCS 8
Stefan, Jennifer 55
Steiner, Casey 68
systems thinking/thinkers 11–14, 20n25, 22, 41, 49, 70

Taxpayer's Night (2008), Baltimore City Council 134
technical reform approach 4, 18n8
three-skill approach to leadership 13–14
top-down approach (district-/state-mandated) 7–8. *see also* bottom-up approach
traditional model 35–37
21st Century Community Learning Centers (21st CCLC) grant Program 113, 129

UCLA Center for Mental Health in Schools & Student/Learning Supports 76
university-assisted community school 30, 81–82, 114

vision, school's 40–48, 50, 55, 62, 66, 81, 87, 92, 114, 157–158; broken-record approach 47–48; community of practice 48–49; and logic model *100*, 100–101; as north star 47; partners' role in 87–88; personal vision 42; shared vision 43, 50; two-step process recommended by researchers 45–46; vision and mission statement 42, 44, 46, 157–158;

Wayne County Full-Service Community Schools Logic Model *105*
Webb Middle School, Austin 126, 167
Wheatley, Margaret 51–52
White, Mary 54
Wilson-Wood, Donette 63
wrap-around services 31–32

For Product Safety Concerns and Information please contact our EU representative GPSR@taylorandfrancis.com
Taylor & Francis Verlag GmbH, Kaufingerstraße 24, 80331 München, Germany